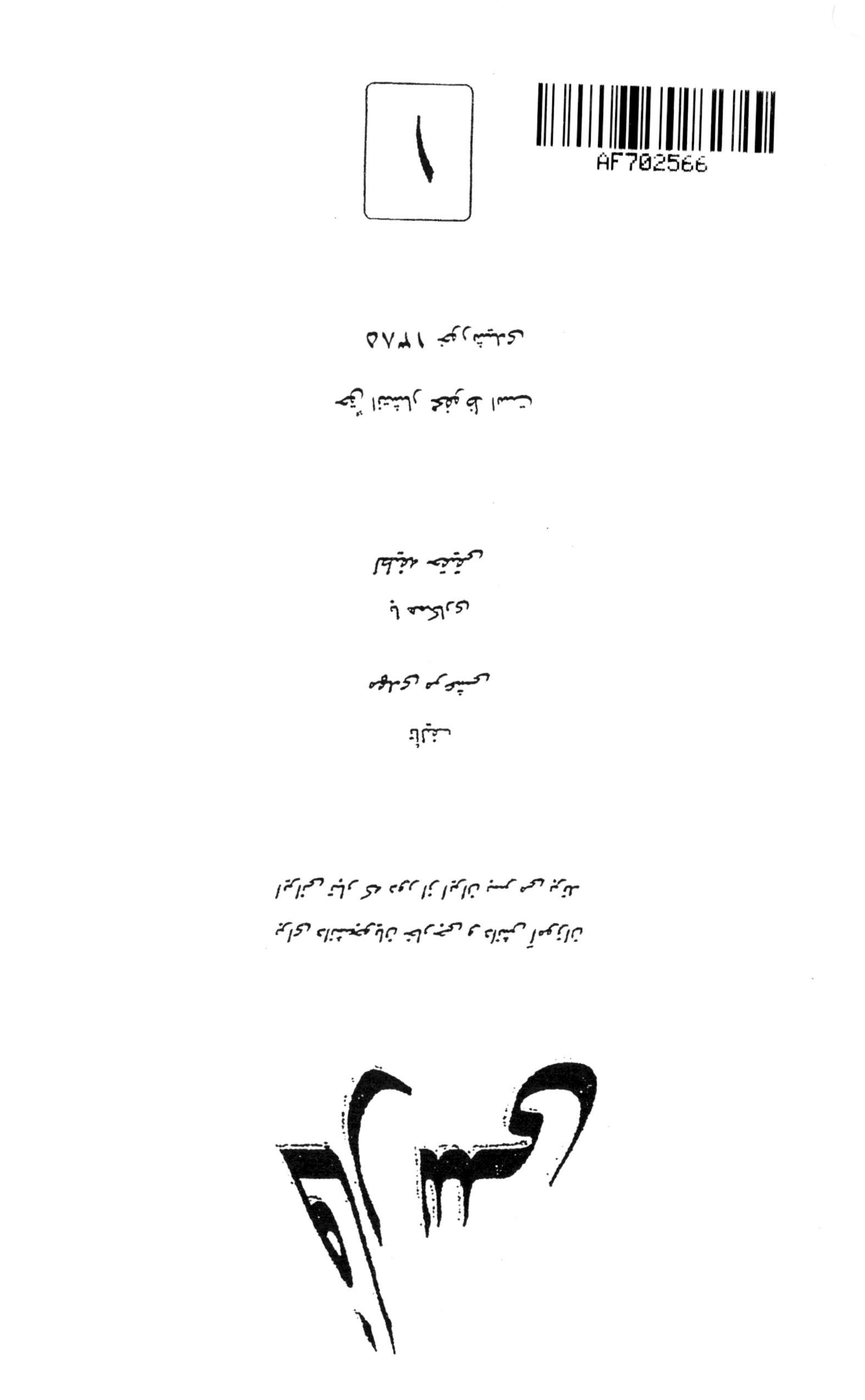

١

[illegible]

[illegible]

[illegible]

[illegible]

[illegible]

[illegible]

[illegible]

[illegible]

[illegible]

آنچه در این کتاب می خوانید

﴿ یادآوری ﴾

درس ها و تمرین های این کتاب روی نوارهای صوتی و ویدیوئی ضبط شده تا یادگیری زبان فارسی را آسانتر و دلپذیرتر نماید. در گفت و شنودها شیوه گفتاری فارسی زبانان و در خواندن و نوشتن تلفظ نوشتاری به کار رفته است. علاوه بر آن در ویدیوها حرکات چشم و ابرو و دست نیز که در گفت و شنود به یاری سخن گویان می آید در خور توجه است. محتوای فرهنگی دروس بردانش و آگاهی دانشجویان می افزاید و آنانرا با دنیای فارسی زبانان آشنا می سازد.

زبان گفتار - زبان نوشتار

Colloquial vs. Standard Written Persian

All dialogues and the Persian script of the dialogues presented in this course highlight a number of differences between spoken and written Persian. In general, Persian speakers employ colloquial (spoken) style in their everyday oral communication. In written communication, however, they mostly use the standard written Persian.

You may find understanding the differences between the two styles of Persian from the beginning a challenging task. However, with systematic practice that are provided in this course you could become accustomed to the natural speed of spoken Persian. Materials that offer unnatural slow-speed speeches may prove inadequate.

The video production of the dialogues portrays authentic models of face to face communication and prepares you to cope with the natural spoken Persian. Different native speakers have recorded the dialogues in colloquial Persian. The script of the dialogues in the standard written Persian will aid you take note of the differences between the two styles.

پیش گفتار

The tables, the English notes and the exercises presented in the first two lessons are primarily intended to provide an introduction to the Persian letters and sounds and serve as a reference guide to the writing system of Persian.

The Persian script CD is designed to provide additional explanations and interactive exercises to the introductory chapter of the book and they complement each other.

Activity 1

Listen to the CD and practice the names of the letters. Try to remember their dictionary order of the letters as they appear in Table 1. Note that the first sound you hear in the name of each letter represents the sound value of that letter. For example, the letters, ن م ل represent the sounds /l/, /m/, and /n/, respectively.

الفبای فارسی

ت	پ	ب	ا
ح	چ	ج	ث
ر	ذ	د	خ
ش	س	ژ	ز
ظ	ط	ض	ص
ق	ف	غ	ع
م	ل	گ	ک
ی	ه	و	ن

Table1. Letters of the Alphabet

Three dots	پ ث چ ژ ش
Two dots	ت ق
One dot	ب ج خ ذ ز ض ظ غ ف ن
No dots	ا ح د ر س ص ط ع ک گ ل م و ه ی

Using Dots to Distinguish Letters

The use of dots is a significant feature for most of the letters. Very often letters which have the same basic shape are distinguished by dots. One, two, or three dots may appear below or above a letter. A few letters do not have any dots.

Activity 2

Practice reading the names of the letters

ترتیب الفبائی	حرفها	نام حرفها
۱	ا	الف
۲	ب	بِ
۳	پ	پِ
۴	ت	تِ
۵	ث	ثِ
۶	ج	جیم
۷	چ	چِ
۸	ح	حِ
۹	خ	خِ
۱۰	د	دال
۱۱	ذ	ذال
۱۲	ر	رِ
۱۳	ز	زِ
۱۴	ژ	ژِ
۱۵	س	سین
۱۶	ش	شین

ترتیب الفبائی	حرفها	نام حرفها
۱۷	ص	صاد
۱۸	ض	ضاد
۱۹	ط	طا
۲۰	ظ	ظا
۲۱	ع	عین
۲۲	غ	غین
۲۳	ف	فِ
۲۴	ق	قاف
۲۵	ک	کاف
۲۶	گ	گاف
۲۷	ل	لام
۲۸	م	میم
۲۹	ن	نون
۳۰	و	واو
۳۱	ه	هِ
۳۲	ی	یِ

Table 2. Names of the letters

حرفهای پیوسته:

ب پ ت ث ج چ ح خ

س ش ص ض ط ظ ع غ

ف ق ک گ ل م ن ه

ی

* * *

حرفهای جدا:

ا د ذ ر ز ژ و

Table 3. Connectors vs. Non-Connectors

Connectors vs. Non-Connectors

The letters can be divided into two distinct categories:***Connectors*** and ***Non*-Connectors**. A connector can join with any following letter, but a non-connector cannot. However, both categories share the common feature of joining any preceding letters.

Activity 3

Listen to and practice reading the following words.

آ

آب

ا

ایران

ب بـ

بَرگ

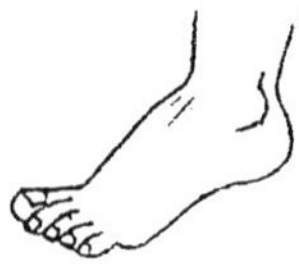

پ پـ

پا

ت تـ

توپ

ث ثـ

ثرَیا

Variant Shapes of the Letters

The number of the variant shapes of the letters differs from each other. Besides the independent form, a non-connector has a variant which occurs when a non-connector links a preceding letter. In handwritten Persian a connector may have four variant shapes. In the printed form, both the connectors and non-connectors are usually reduced to two and one forms, respectively.

ج ﺟ

جوجه

چ ﭼ

چَتر

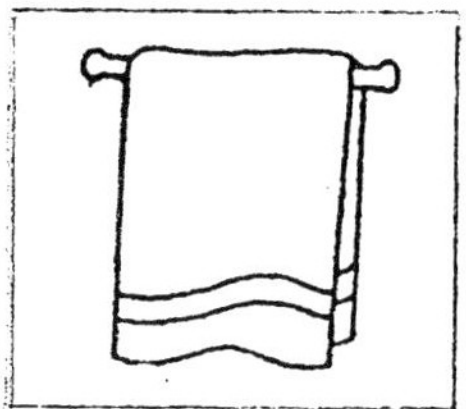

ح ﺣ

حوله

خ ﺧ

خانه

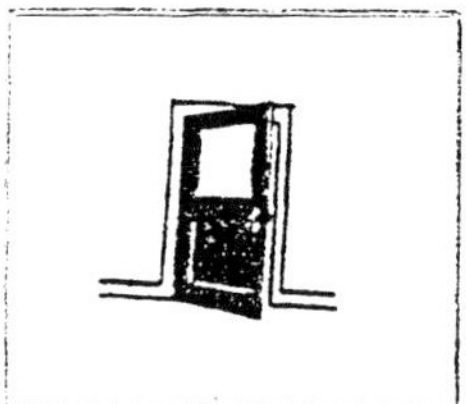

د

دَر

ذ

ذُرت

ر

رادیو

ز

زن

ژ

ژاکت

س سـ

ساعت

ش شـ

شیر

ض ضـ

ضبط صوت

ص صـ

صندلی

ط

طوطی

ظ

ظُهر

ع ع

عینک

غ غ

غاز

ف ف

فارسی

ق ق

قَلَم

ک ک

کت

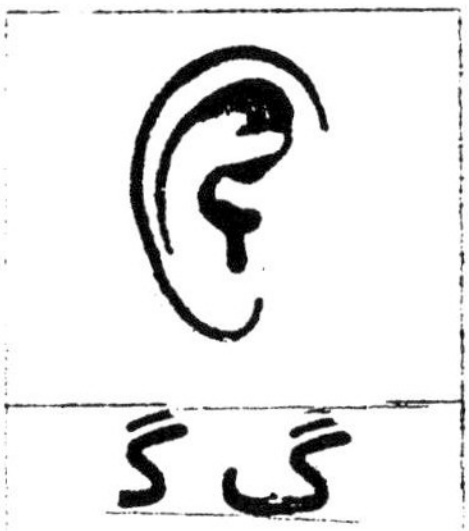

گ گ

گوش

ل ل

لَب

م م

میز

ن ن

نادِر

و

ویلن

ه ه

هَواپیما

ی ی

یاسمین

حرفهای همانند

۱− ب پ ت ث ن ی

۲− ج چ ح خ

۳− د ذ ر ز ژ و

۴− س ش

۵− ص ض ط ظ

۶− ع غ

۷− ف ق

۸− ا ک گ ل

Table 4. Similar letters

Similar Letters

Notice that the members of each of the following groups, in most cases, are similar in their basic shapes, but may slightly differ according to their position in a word. In group 1, for example, the letters ب ن ی are similar only in their initial and medial positions to other members of the group.

نشانه ها در خط فارسی

۱– زبر   َ

۲– زیر   ِ

۳– پیش   ُ

۴– مد   آ

۵– همزه   ء

۶– تنوین   اً

۷– تشدید   ّ

۸– سکون   ْ

Special Signs

In addition to the thirty two letters of the alphabet, there are eight special signs occasionally used in writing to assist the reader in correctly identifying and pronouncing the words. The vowels signs and سکون are hardly ever used, especially in printing.

1. The first three signs are used to indicate the presence of the vowels /a/, /e/ and /o/ in a word. For example.

notebook	دَفتَر
pencil	مِداد
professor	اُستاد

2. The sign مد occurs over the letter الف , and the combination is pronounced /ā/ as in:

water	آب
fire	آتش
Ādam	آدم

Unlike other special signs, مد is not generally omitted in writing. In certain wotrds the absence of مد , versus its presence change the meaning and pronunciation of the words, e.g.,

property	مال	result	مَآل
eyebrow	ابرو	honor	آبرو
A monetary unit	قران	The Qurān	قرآن

3. The environments in which the sign همزه may appear include the following:

a. The glottal stop preceded by the vowel /o/, e.g.,

dream	رؤیا
question	سؤال
author	مؤلف

b. The glottal stop preceded by the vowel /a/, e.g.,

vote	رأی
delay	تأخیر
effect	تأثیر

c. The glottal stop in the final position, e.g.,

evil	سوء
portion	جزء
object	شئ

d. The glottal stop in the middle of a word, e.g.,

chief	رئیس
responsible	مسئول
newspapers	جرائد (جراید)

4. The sign تنوین represents "nunation" (giving the ن), which is an /n/ sound at the end of a word. The letter الف is written at the end of the word to hold the sign تنوین. The sign serves to designate Arabic words used in Persian with the meaning of adverbs.

recently	اخیراً
usually	معمولاً
approximately	تقریباً

5. The sign تشدید indicates "gemination" (the doubling of a consonant) within a word.

but	امّا
pronunciation	تلفّظ
carpenter	نجّار

6. The sign سکون indicates the absence of a vowel sound after the consonant above which it stands. In other words, it indicates that there is no vowel separating two consonants in a word, e.g.,

cold	سرْما

نشانه ها در خط فارسی

زبر	زیر	پیش
ـَـ	ـِـ	ـُـ

مدّ	همزه	تنوین	تشدید	سکون
~	ء	ً	ّ	°

Table 5. Special Signs

حروف عربی

معنی	کلمات عربی	حروف	#
one third	ثلث	ث	١
arithmetic	حساب	ح	٣
page	صفحه	ص	٣
drum	ضرب	ض	۴
nature	طبیعت	ط	۵
noon	ظهر	ظ	۶
excellent	عالی	ع	٧
judge	قاضی	ق	٨

Table 6. The Arabic Letters

The eight letters listed in Table 6 are peculiar to Arabic and they are not found in words of Persian origin. In Arabic these letters represent distinct consonants. Arabic loan words are spelled as in Arabic. However, no distinction is observed in pronunciation by speakers of Persian. (See page 2 for additional data.)

حروف همخوان

1. One letter < - > One Sound

Most of the letters in the Persian alphabet correspond to one sound, and one sound only, in the English alphabet. The list of these letters is as follows.

English equivalent	sounds	letters	#
boy	/b/	ب	۱
pot	/p/	پ	۲
jar	/j/	ج	۳
cheese	/č/	چ	۴
n/a	/x/	خ	۵
day	/d/	د	۶
road	/r/	ر	۷
pleasure	/ž/	ژ	۸
shoes	/š/	ش	۹
fire	/f/	ف	۱۰
n/a	/q/	ق	۱۱
key	/k/	ک	۱۲
gas	/g/	گ	۱۳
lip	/l/	ل	۱۴
man	/m/	م	۱۵
noon	/n/	ن	۱۶

Table 7. One letter <-> One Sound

حروف همصوت

2. Multiple Letters < - > One Sound

There are certain letters that have distinctive sound values in Arabic. When these letters appear in words of Arabic origin the sounds change into sounds that already exist in Persian. For example, the consonants ت and ط in Arabic are distinct from one another. However, in Persian, the two letters represent the sound /t/. Other examples of this type are listed in the following table.

#	letters	sounds	examples
۱	ه	/h/	weather هوا
	ح		condition حال
۲	ت	/t/	blade تیغ
	ط		drum طبل
۳	غ	/q/	food غذا
	ق		boat قایق
۴	الف	/’/	delay تأخیر
	ع		picture عکس
۵	ث	/s/	one third ثلث
	س		green سبز
	ص		morning صبح
۶	ذ	/z/	corn ذرّت
	ز		yellow زرد
	ض		drum ضرب
	ظ		noon ظهر

Table 8. Multiple Letters < - > One Sound

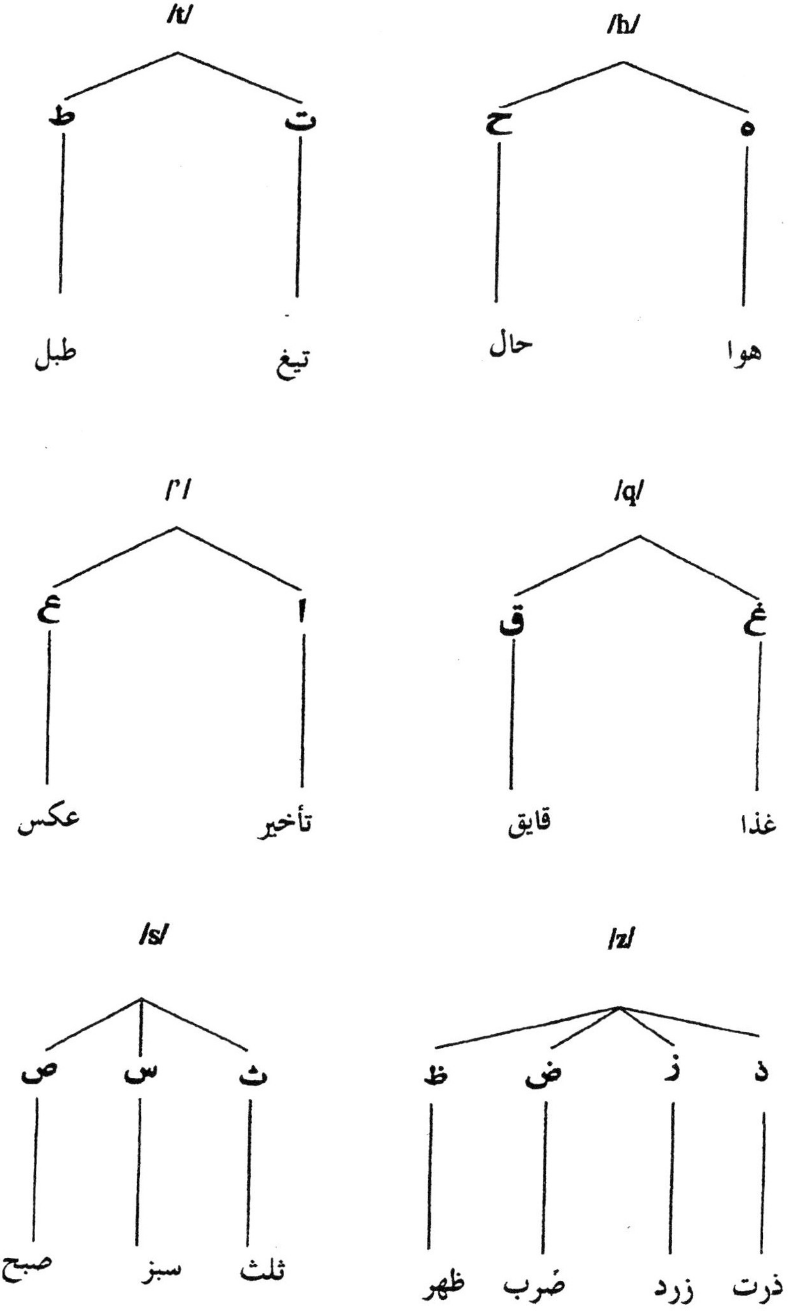
/h/
ه
ح
هوا
حال
/t/
ت
ط
تیغ
طبل
/q/
غ
ق
غذا
قایق
/'/
ا
ع
تأخیر
عکس
/z/
ذ
ز
ض
ظ
ذرت
زرد
ضَرب
ظهر
/s/
ث
س
ص
ثلث
سبز
صبح

حروف چند صوتی

3. One Letter < - > Multiple Sounds

There are four letters in the alphabet that may represent either vowels or consonants. Note the double function of the letter ه in the word همسایه 'neighbor' where the letter stands for two types of sounds. The initial letter has the sound value of the consonant /h/, and the final letter represents the vowel /e/. In the case of و and ی it should be noted that these letters may represent vowels, consonants, and semivowels as illustrated in the following table.

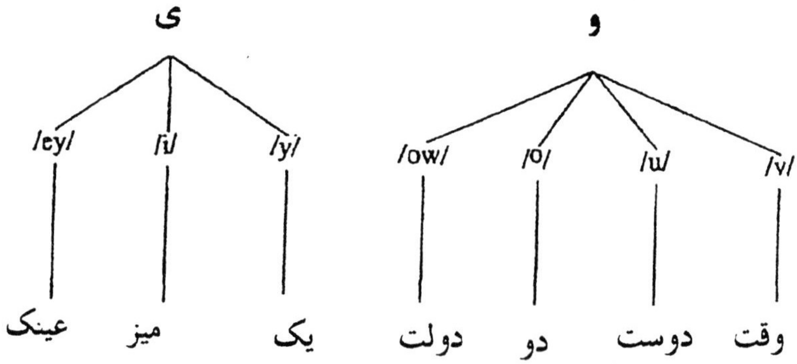

#	Letters	Sounds	Words
1	الف	/ā/ /'/	پا رأس
2	ه	/h/ /e/	هوا خانه
3	ی	/y/ /i/ /ey/	یک میز عینک
4	و	/v/ /u/ /o/ /ow/	وقت دوست دو دولت

Table 9. One Letter < - > Multiple Sounds

املای واکه ها

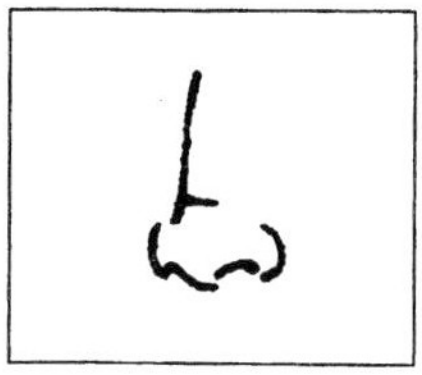

۱- بینی

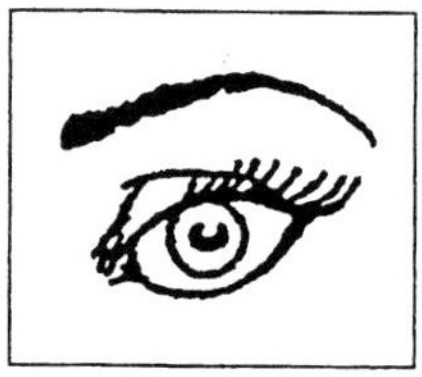

۲ - چشم

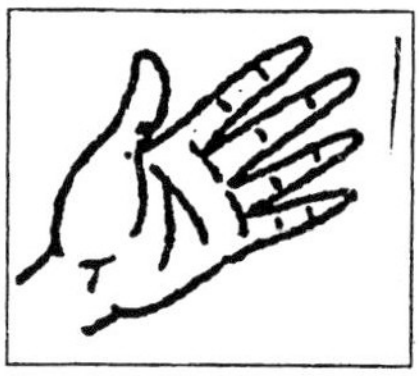

۳- دَست

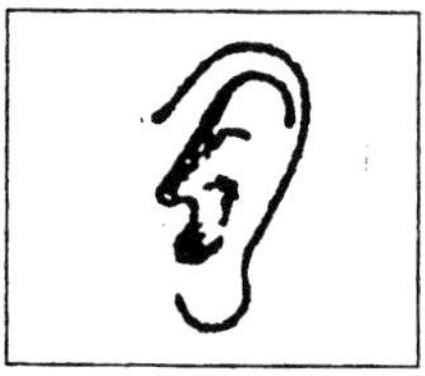

۴-گوش

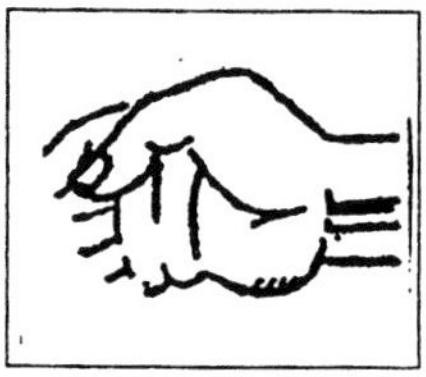

۵- مُچ

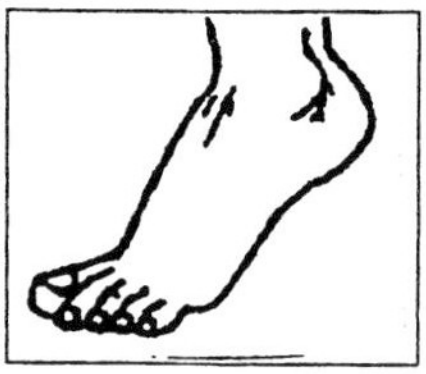

۶- پا

The Spelling of Vowels

Modern Persian has six vowels. These sounds function as the peaks of syllables. Not all Persian vowels appear in the spelling of words. The letters الف و ی are used in writing to represent the vowels /ā/, /u/ and /i/ as in the words listed above. Note that the vowels /a/, /e/ and /o/ do not appear in spelling. They may be marked by special signs. The signs are usually not inserted in writing except when necessary to assist the reader in correctly pronouncing the words.

Activity 5

Write 'T' for true and 'F' for false in the blank spaces.

a. _____ Persian is written from right to left.

b. _____ There are 26 letters in the Persian alphabet.

c. _____ Numerals are written from left to right.

d. _____ Connectors always connect to the letter that occurs after them.

e. _____ Non-connectors do not have initial and medial forms.

f. _____ In addition to the letters, there are eight special signs.

g. _____ The special signs are usually omitted in written Persian.

h. _____ The printed style is different from the handwritten style.

i. _____ Most letters in the Persian alphabet represent consonants.

j. _____ Certain letters have the same basic shape but are distinguished by the number and position of dots.

k. _____ There are no capital letters in Persian.

i. _____ The letters ی و الف represent three vowels.

Activity 6

Fill in the blanks with the Persian letters that corresponds to The English sounds listed below.

1. /b/	2. /m/	3./k/
4. /l/	5. /r/	6. /j/
7. /g/	8. /p/	9. /u/
10. /n/	11. /ā/	12. /f/
13. /i/	14. /v/	15. /q/
16. /š/	17. /d/	18. /h/

Activity 7

Reading with Flashcards

Have flashcards 1-12 ready. Listen to the CD and repeat what you hear on the disk. Try to follow the steps indicated below in the reading practice.

1 Look at the Persian word that appears on one side of the flashcard.

2 Identify the letters and spell the word. In spelling each word, pronounce the names of the letters.

3 Read the word.

4 Look at the other side of the card for the matching picture or English equivalent of the word.

Activity 8

Fill in the blanks with the independent forms of the letters.

	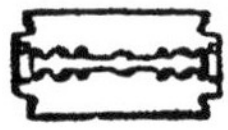		
۴	۳	۲	۱
	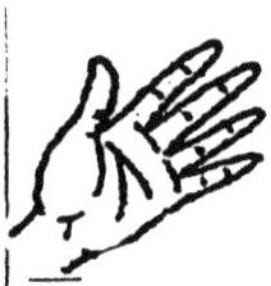	ا	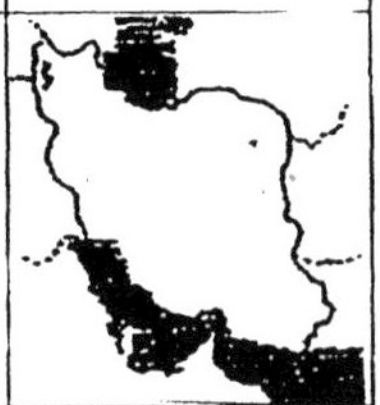
۸	۷	۶	۵
			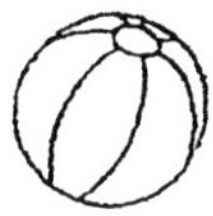
		۱۰	۹

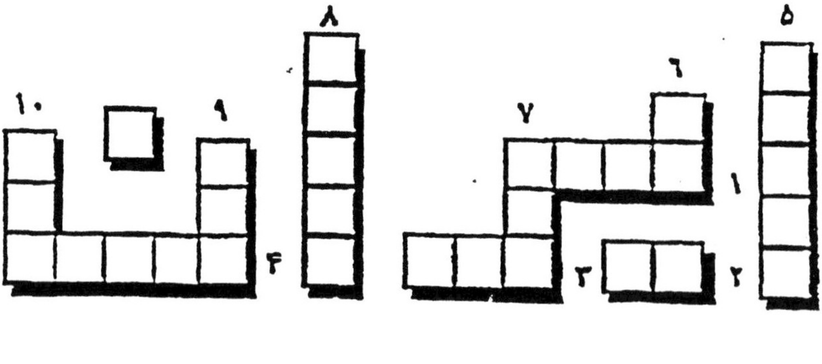

سلام و احوالپرسی

Greetings

پرویز سلام.

مریم سلام.

پرویز حالتان چطور است؟

مریم خوب است، مرسی.

حالِ شما چطور است؟

پرویز بد نیست، متشکّرم.

Leave-taking

پرویز خداحافظ .

مریم بسلامت.

Additional Expressions

صبح بخیر!

شب بخیر!

لطفِ شما زیاد.

استاد	**آقا، اِسمِ شما چیست؟**
پرویز	**اِسمِ من پرویز است.**
استاد	**شما ایرانی هستید؟**
پرویز	**بله، من ایرانی هستم.**
استاد	**شما فارسی می دانید؟**
پرویز	**بله، فارسی می دانم.**
استاد	**انگلیسی چطور؟**
پرویز	**انگلیسی هم می دانم.**
استاد	**اسم آن آقا چیست؟**
پرویز	**اسم ایشان رابرت است.**
استاد	**رابرت آمریکائی است ؟**
پرویز	**بله، ایشان آمریکائی است.**
استاد	**ایشان فارسی می داند؟**
پرویز	**بله، کمی فارسی می داند.**
استاد	**عربی هم می داند؟**
پرویز	**نخیر، عربی نمی داند.**

من ایرانی هستم	ما ایرانی هستیم
تو ایرانی هستی	شما ایرانی هستید
پرویز ایرانی است	پرویز و مریم ایرانی هستند

تمرین خواندن

Reading with Flashcards

Have flashcards 1-12 ready. Listen to the CD and repeat what you hear. Try to follow the steps indicated below in the reading practice.

1. Look at the Persian word that appears on one side of the flashcard.
2. Identify the letters and spell the word. In spelling each word, pronounce the names of the letters.
3. Read the word.
4. Look at the other side of the card for the matching picture or English equivalent of the word.

برای فراگیری الفبا و تمرین خواندن

Flashcards

For active recall of vocabulary and practice on recognition of letters of the alphabet and spelling, Persian flashcards have been designed. They serve as word cues in oral drills, but they may be used for review purposes as well. The easiest and most common use of these cards is to "flash" them briefly for the class to read.

کِتاب

۱

دَفتَر

۲

مِداد

۳

میز

۴

صندلی

۵

تخته سیاه

۶

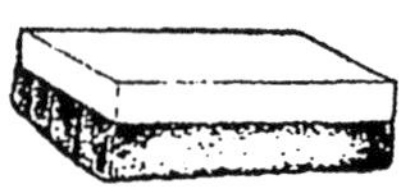

پاک کُن

۷

گَچ

۸

ساعت

۹

پرسش:

این کتاب کیست؟	این کتاب من است.
این مداد کیست؟	این مداد مریم است.
آن دفتر کیست؟	آن دفتر بیژن است.

کی + است ⟵ کیست

ساعت

کلید

کت

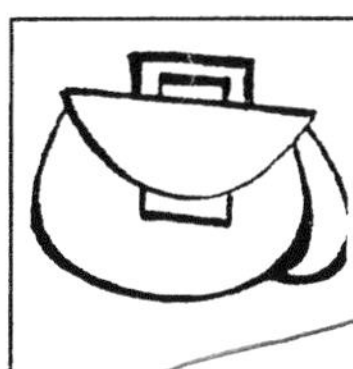

کیف

قلم

عینک

معنی انگلیسی	کلمه‌های تازه
window	پَنجره
open	باز
closed	بَسته
near	نَزدیک
under	زیر
behind	پُشت
history	تاریخ
room	اتاق
laboratory	آزمایشگاه
watch, hour	ساعت
key	کلید
girl, daughter	دختر
boy, son	پسر
today	امروز
to read	خواندَن
to know (something)	دانستن (دان)
to know (somebody)	شناختن (شناس)
to have	داشتن (دار)

گفتگو

در کلاس درس

این، چیست؟ آن، کتاب است.

این، چیست؟ آن، دفتر است.

این، مداد است؟ بله، آن، مداد است.

این هم مداد است؟ نخیر، آن مداد نیست.

گچ است.

این چیست؟ این، میز است.

این، چیست؟ آن صندلی است.

این هم صندلی است؟ بله.

این،میز است یاصندلی؟

این، میز است.

کتاب

دفتر

گچ

میز

صندلی

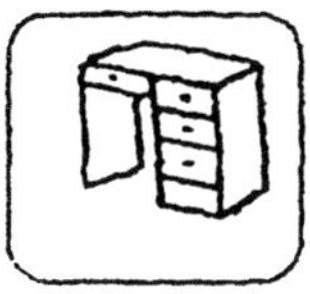

میز

تخته سیاه

دیوار

مداد کجاست؟

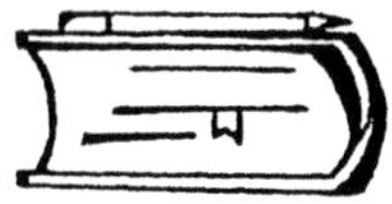

مداد روی کتاب است.

مداد زیر کتاب است.

مداد پشت کتاب است.

مداد نزدیک کتاب است.

پرسش:

آن چیست؟ — آن کتاب است.

آن کتابِ کیست؟ — آن کتاب من است.

اِسم کتاب شما چیست؟ — اسم آن تاریخِ ایران است.

کتاب شما کجاست؟ — روی میز است.

کتاب پرویز کجاست؟ — کتاب او زیر میز است

چه (چی) + است ← چیست
که(کی) + است ← کیست

تمرین خواندن

استاد این ، چیست؟

دانشجو این، پنجره است.

استاد پنجره ، باز است؟

دانشجو نخیر باز نیست.بسته است.

پنجره

استاد آن، در است یا دیوار؟

دانشجو آن، در است.

استاد در بسته است؟

دانشجو بله، بسته است.

در

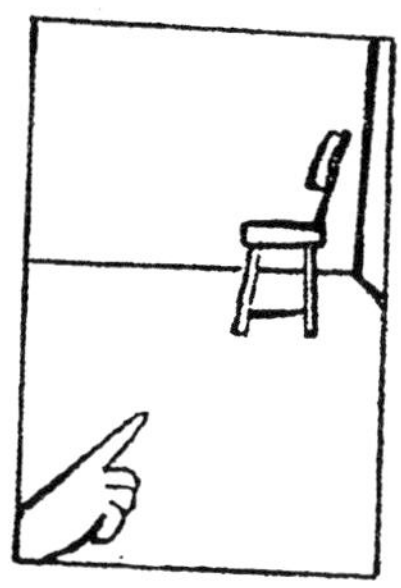

استاد آن، صندلی است؟

دانشجو بله، صندلی است.

استاد آن صندلی، نزدیک دیواراست؟

دانشجو بله، نزدیک دیوار است.

صندلی

تمرین خواندن

۱ـ

سوسن: آن، کتاب شماست؟

آرش: بله، آن کتاب من است.

سوسن: کتابتان روی صندلی است؟

آرش: بله، روی صندلی است.

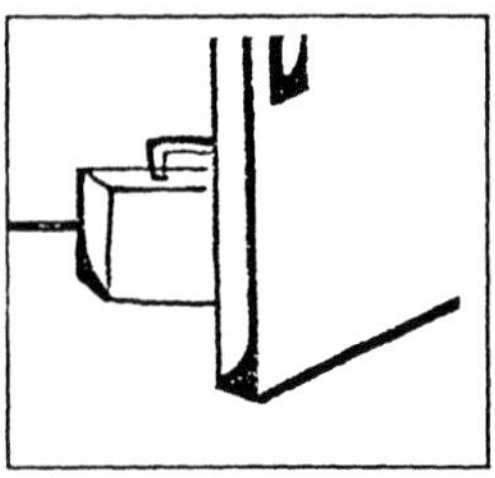

۲ـ

سوسن: آن، کیف کیست؟

آرش: کیف استاد است.

سوسن: کیف استاد کجاست؟

آرش: پشت در است.

۳ـ

سوسن: اسم آن پسر چیست؟

آرش: اسمش کوروش است.

سوسن: کوروش، کجاست؟

آرش: در آزمایشگاه زبان است.

۴ـ

سوسن: اسم آن آقا چیست؟

آرش: آقای براون است.

سوسن: آقای براون استاد انگلیسی است؟

آرش: بله، ایشان استاد انگلیسی ماست.

۵ـ

سوسن آن چیست؟

آرش آن تلفن است.

سوسن تلفن زیر صندلی است؟

آرش نخیر، روی صندلی است.

۶ـ

سوسن آن آقا ایرانی است؟

آرش نخیر، ایشان آمریکائی است.

سوسن اسم ایشان چیست؟

آرش آقای هریسن است.

سوسن آقای هریسن استاد شیمی است؟

آرش بله، ایشان استاد شیمی است.

کلمه‌های تازه	معنی انگلیسی
فردا	tomorrow
ساختمان	building
نوار	tape
گوش کردن	to listen
دوره کردن	to review
کمک کردن	to help
شماره	number
کدام	which
تلفظ	pronunciation
آنجا	over there
لغات	vocabulary
کتابخانه	library
مدرسه	school

گوشی

۱

نوار کاست

۲

ضبط صوت

۳

خواندن

در کلاس انگلیسی

پرویز و مریم فردا کلاس انگلیسی دارند. کلاس انگلیسی در اتاق شماره ۲۵ است. استاد انگلیسی پرویز و مریم آمریکائی است. اسم ایشان خانم الیزابت براون است. کلاس انگلیسی دوازده تا دانشجو دارد، هشت تا دختر و چهار تا پسر.

پرسش:

۱ـ استاد انگلیسی مریم ایرانی است یا آمریکائی؟

۲ـ اسم استاد انگلیسی ایشان چیست؟

۳ـ کلاس انگلیسی چند تا دانشجو دارد؟

٤ـ پرویز و مریم امروز کلاس دارند یا فردا؟

۵ـ کلاس انگلیسی در کدام اتاق است؟

خواندن

در آزمایشگاه زبان

ما فردا ساعت ده آزمایشگاه زبان داریم. آزمایشگاه زبان مدرسه ما در اتاق شماره ۱۲ ساختمان کتابخانه است. ما در آزمایشگاه زبان به نوار کاست گوش می کنیم و لغات، خواندن و گفتگو را در آنجا دوره می کنیم. تمرین در آزمایشگاه به تلفظ فارسی ما خیلی کمک می کند.

پرسش:

۱ـ شما کی آزمایشگاه زبان دارید؟

۲ـ آزمایشگاه مدرسه شما در کدام ساختمان است؟

۳ـ آزمایشگاه زبان در کدام اتاق است؟

٤ـ در آزمایشگاه زبان چکار می کنید؟

۵ـ تمرین در آزمایشگاه به فارسی شما کمک می کند؟

یادداشتهای انگلیسی

Greetings

سلام is a greeting used at any time of the day. It corresponds to the English 'good morning, good afternoon, good day, hi and hello.' In response to سلام , the same expression may be used.

A handshake is the customary greeting. A single bow or nod while shaking hands shows respect. When asked حالتان چطور است؟ , an Iranian politely says متشکرم 'thank you' and then, خوب است I am fine.

Leave-taking Expressions

A common leave-taking expression is خدا حافظ 'May God protect you'. In response, one of the following expressions may be used.

خداحافظ

بسلامت

لطف شما زیاد

خدا نگهدار

Titles of Address

In formal conversation, Iranians often use titles of address. Titles precede family names. In informal introductions, family names and titles are not mentioned. However, in formal introductions when two people are introduced by a third person, titles, the first and the family names are given.

The following is a list of titles used in Persian.

دکتر is used to address medical doctors and university professors who have earned a doctorate.

استاد is used to address a college or university instructor.

- خانم 'Mrs. or Miss' is used with the first and family names of a female. The title usually follows the first name. However, it precedes the family name as in the following examples.

  a) with first names پروین خانم

  b) with family names خانم آزادی

  c) with first and family names خانم پروین آزادی

- The titles may also be used without a personal name. For example:

  خانم، حالتان چطور است؟

  ببخشید آقا، اسم شما چیست؟

- The title دوشیزه is used for single young woman in formal communication

  دوشیزه مهین راد

- آقا 'Mr.' precedes the family name, but follows the first names when fami name is not used. For examples:

  a) with family names آقای آزادی

  b) with first and family names آقای احمد آزادی

  c) with first names احمد آقا

  In general, titles of address are used in polite and formal communication. However, close friends, immediate members of family, and children usuall each other by their first names.

- Professional titles such as دکتر , مهندس , رئیس , etc. are used in combinatio with the titles آقا and خانم as in the following examples.

  خانم دکتر محمودی

  خانم مهندس نادری

  آقای رئیس دانشگاه

Pronunciation

In order for students to get off to a good start in Persian pronunciation, distinctive vowels should be identified, perceived, and produced accurately. Reduction of vowels, which applies very regularly in English pronunciation, should be avoided in Persian. In dealing with vowels one must first learn how one vowel is distinguished from others so that it will not be mistaken for any other vowels. The description of vowels may not be the answer to the problems of pronunciation. The best way to improve pronunciation is by listening to and imitating native speakers of Persian.

Vowels

Modern Persian has six vowels, all of which appeared in the first dialogue. These sounds function as the peaks of syllables. Note the occurrence of the vowels in the following words.

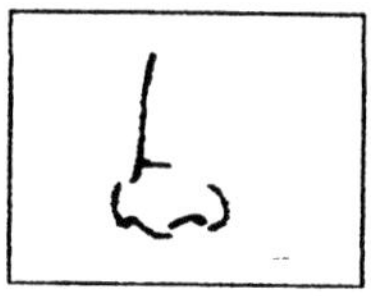

۱ـ بینی

۲ـ چشم

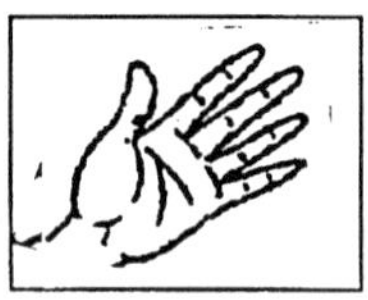

۳ـ دَست

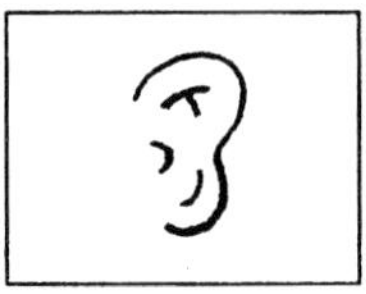

٤ـ گوش

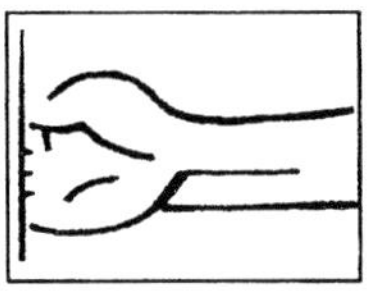

٥ـ مچ

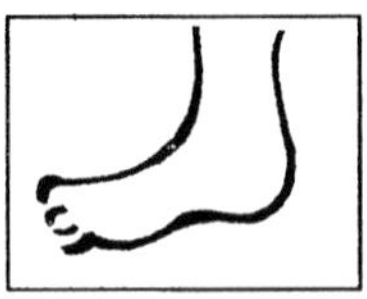

٦ـ پا

Colloquial vs. Written Persian

How do you pronounce the following sentences in colloquial Persian? Apply the rules indicated below. Change the following.

1. است —> /e/.
2. The vowel /ā/ —> /u/ before /n/.

حالتان چطور است؟	۱
خوب است.	۲
حال شما چطور است؟	۳
این چیست؟	۴
آن میز است.	۵
این صندلی است؟	۶
این مداد است یا گچ؟	۷
آن هم مداد است؟	۸
نخیر، آن مداد نیست، کتاب است.	۹

Word Stress

In words of more than one syllable the stressed syllable stands out by pronunciation and is heard louder than unstressed syllables in the word. In general, word stress falls on the last syllable of non-verbal including nouns, adjectives, prepositions and adverbs. Words with the stress on the first syllable are limited in number.

Diphthongs

The most common diphthongs in Persian are /ey/ as in میمون 'monkey' and /ow/ as in دولت 'government'. To pronounce the diphthong /ey/ begin with the vowel /e/ and then add the semivowel /y/ after /e/ gliding smoothly from /e/ to /i/ making the sound /ey/.

میمون

chimpanzee

میدان

square

To pronounce the semivowel /ow/ start with the vowel /o/, and then glide away to /v/ with the lips being slightly rounded. Words that contain the diphthong /ow/ include:

دولت

government

دوره

review

The less common diphthongs in Persian is /āy/ as in

نای

windpipe

چای

tea

دستور زبان

Personal Pronouns

There are two sets of personal pronouns in Persian: independent pronouns and suffixed pronouns. The two sets of the pronouns have the following forms.

Independent Pronouns

ما	من
شما	تو
ایشان	او

Note:

1. The first person singular من , followed by the post-position را is written together as مرا whereby من loses its final letter. The combination is spelled and pronounced مرا . In colloquial Persian, the first person plural ما though plural, may take the plural suffix ها , to express 'all of us'.

2. In conversation, the secondary plural may occur with شما to denote 'all of you'. Like its English equivalent, شما is used for one person or more than one person. The second person singular تو 'thou' is used mostly among close friends, members of the family, and in addressing God. The combination of تو and the post-position را has the alternate spelling of ترا.

3. A third person singular distinction is made between human, on the one hand, and inanimate on the other. The pronoun او is used for both 'he' and 'she', and آن for objects and animals. In the polite style of the language ایشان 'they' may refer to 'he' or 'she'. While ایشان is exclusively used for persons, آنها may refer to objects, animals, and persons.

4. In general, the independent pronouns are not used as frequently as their equivalents in English because in Persian, verb endings denote the number and persons of the verb. Thus, the subject pronouns are omitted in Persian, unless special emphasis has to be made.

Suffixed Pronouns

Suffixed pronouns, unlike independent pronouns are not words by themselves. They are attached to their preceding words and are considered part of them. Following is the list of suffixed pronouns.

– م	– مان
– ت	– تان
– ش	– شان

Note:

1. All suffixed pronouns begin with a vowel. For the singular pronouns the initial vowel is pronounced /a/ in written Persian and /e/ in spoken Persian..

2. Suffixed pronouns do not receive stress. However, when a pronoun has to receive stress in a sentence, the independent form of the pronoun is used as in the example illustrated below.

۱ـ آقای نادری، حالتان چطور است؟

۲– خوب است، متشکّرم. حال شما چطور است؟

Notice that in sentence 1, Mr. Naderi is using شما and not the corresponding suffixed pronoun تان –because of implied emphasis and contrast in the second question.

3. In written Persian, when the suffixed pronouns are attached to words ending in the vowels /a/ or /u/, the letter ی is inserted between the word and the suffixed pronoun. For example:

پایم	پایمان
پایت	پایتان
پایش	پایشان

مویم	مویمان
مویت	مویتان
مویش	مویشان

Note:

In colloquial Persian, the letter ی and the initial vowel of the suffixed pronoun are dropped altogether. In the plural forms, the final vowel /ā/ is pronounced /u/ because the vowel /ā/ precedes the nasal consonant /n/.

If a word ends in the vowel /e/ the glottal stop is inserted. In spelling the letter الف is used in this environment as shown in the following examples:

. خانه ام   نامه ات   همسایه اش

4. In spoken Persian, the suffixed pronouns are more commonly used than the independent pronouns. The suffixed pronouns are attached to different parts of speech, including nouns, adjectives, adverbs, prepositions and verbs. For example:

الف– (اسم + ضمیر پیوسته)	برادرم
ب – (صفت + ضمیر پیوسته)	برادر کوچکم
ج – (قید + ضمیر پیوسته)	بالایش
د–(حرف اضافه + ضمیر پیوسته)	اَزَت (از تو)
ه – (فعل + ضمیر پیوسته)	دیدمش

Verb Endings

In Persian the agreement between the subject and the verb (in person and number) is marked in the form of verb endings. These endings are suffixed to all verb stems, with one exception. The third person singular of the past stem takes no ending. The paradigm below illustrates the form of the verb endings.

the simple present tense

می خوانم	می خوانیم
می خوانی	می خوانید
می خواند	می خوانند

the simple past

خواندم	خواندیم
خواندی	خواندید
خواند	خواندند

Note:

1. In written Persian, the ending of the third person singular, present tense, is pronounced /ad/. In conversation, the pronunciation changes to /e/.

2. The verb endings, except in the third person singular, coincide in form with the short form of "to be". In function, meaning, and their position in the sentence the two elements are distinct.

Types of Sentences

Statements

A simple statement in Persian begins with the subject, which may be one or more than one word. The subject tells us who or what is being talked about. The second part of a sentence is the predicate, which expresses actions or some other kind of event. The predicate contains a verb or a verb phrase that normally appears at the end of the sentence. The right column below lists the kind of elements that may function as the subject, and the left column is the predicate of the sentences.

predicate	subject	
حالا کلاس داریم.	---	۱
حالا کلاس داریم.	ما	۲
انگلیسی می داند.	نادر	۳
انگلیسی می داند.	او	۴
آمریکائی است.	خانم براون	۵
فارسی و فرانسه می داند.	---	۶

Sentences with no overt subject may require comment. In sentence ۱., for example حالا کلاس فارسی داریم the verb ending یم points to the understood subject ما. Thus, it is reasonable to assume that the above sentence is derived from ما حالا کلاس فارسی داریم .

Patterns of Statements

Persian statements fall into patterns, and the number of patterns is quite small. The following sentences illustrate a number of common patterns of statements in Persian The basic patterns will be introduced briefly at this point Details and more discussion will be presented later.

Pattern 1: subject + complement + بودن

استاد فارسی ما ایرانی است.

اسم ایشان خانم پرویزی است.

Notice that in the above pattern, the subject is not the performer of any action. 'To be' is often called a linking verb because it links the predicate very closely to the subject. A linking verb takes a complement. The complement, which precedes the verb to be always refers to the same subject, and it may be may be a noun, an adverbial, a prepositional phrase or an adjective. The formula below shows the predicate patterns with the verb 'to be' in Persian.

Predicate

<u>Subject</u> + { N / Adv / PP / Adj } + بودن

(In this formula N stands for nouns, pronouns or noun phrases; Adj for adjectives; PP for prepositional phrases; and Adv for adverbs.)

Study the following sentences and underline the predicative in each sentence. Then indicate which of the four categories mentioned in pattern 1 is used as the compliment of the verb 'to be'.

کلاس انگلیسی در کدام اتاق است؟ کلاس انگلیسی در اتاق شماره ۲۵ است. استاد انگلیسی ما آمریکائی است. اسم ایشان خانم الیزابت براون است. خانه ایشان نزدیک دانشگاه است.

تمرین و تکلیف

A. Mark the first omitted vowel in the following words, using the special sig

۱ـ سلام	۸ـ خداحافظ
۲ـ چطور	۹ـ بسلامت
۳ـ است	۱۰ـ شب
٤ـ شما	۱۱ـ صبح
٥ـ بد	۱۲ـ لطف
٦ـ کت	۱۳ـ عینک
۷ـ کتاب	١٤ـ قلم

Insert تشدید، مدّ or تنوین in the following words.

۱– اول ۲– اقا ۳– متشکرم ۴– امریکا

۵– ان ۶– تقریبا ۷– محمد ۸– اریا

Reading with Flashcards

Practice reading flashcards 13-26. Follow the steps indicated in the previous exercise- identify the letters, pronounce the names of the letters, then read the words.

B. Write "T" for true and "F" for false.

1_______ In addition to the letters, there are eight special signs which are occasionally used in Persian.

2_______ the sign مد occurs only above the letter الف.

3_______ the signs for the vowels /a/, /e/ and /o/ are usually omitted in writing.

4_______ the sign تنوین is pronounced ان at the end of adverbs.

5_______ the sign همزه shows the absence of a vowel.

6_______ the sign سکون represents the vowel /o/.

7_______ the sign تشدید represents doubling of a consonant.

8_______ in general, special signs are inserted to assist the reader in correct pronunciation and meaning of the words.

C. Read the following numerals.

۱۵ ۱۴ ۱۳ ۱۲ ۱۱

۲۰ ۱۹ ۱۸ ۱۷ ۱۶

یازده دوازده سیزده چهارده پانزده

شانزده هفده هجده نوزده بیست

D. Match each sound with one of the four Persian letters listed below.

1. /b/

☐ ب

☐ ت

☐ ج

☐ د

2. /k/

☐ گ

☐ ل

☐ ک

☐ ر

3. /r/

☐ ر

☐ ذ

☐ س

☐ ژ

4. /i/

☐ و

☐ ی

- ☐ آ
- ☐ ا

5. /l/

- ☐ م
- ☐ د
- ☐ ل
- ☐ ش

6. /m/

- ☐ م
- ☐ ل
- ☐ چ
- ☐ ث

7. /ā/

- ☐ ی
- ☐ و
- ☐ س
- ☐ آ

8. /p/
- ☐ و
- ☐ ی
- ☐ آ
- ☐ پ

9. /d/
- ☐ د
- ☐ و
- ☐ س
- ☐ آ

10. /f/
- ☐ و
- ☐ ی
- ☐ ف
- ☐ ا

11. /q/

- ☐ ی
- ☐ ق
- ☐ س
- ☐ ف

12. /š/

- ☐ چ
- ☐ ی
- ☐ ش
- ☐ پ

E. The Number of Syllables

How many syllables do you hear in the following words? Write the numbers in the blank spaces.

___	سلام	۱
___	چطور	۲
___	خوب	۳
___	متشکّرم	۴
___	شما	۵
___	خداحافظ	۶
___	بسلامت	۷

Word Stress*

In words of more than one syllable the stressed syllable stands out by pronunciation and is heard louder than unstressed syllables. In general, word stress falls on the last syllable of non-verbal including nouns, adjectives, prepositions and adverbs. Words with the stress on the first syllable are limited in number.

Pronounce the following words and underline the strongest syllable. Mark only one syllable for each word.

1. /sa-lām/
2. /ha-le-tun/
3. /šo-mā/
4. /be-sa-lā-mat/
5. /če-towr/
6. /ba-le/
7. /tax-te-si-yāh/
8. /di-vār/
9. /daf-tar/
10. /na-xeyr/
11. /da-neš-ju/

Note that Persian words have a definite place for the stress. Placing stress on t wrong syllable may cause difficulty in recognizing the word.

* See the English notes in the subsequent lesson for more observations on word stress in Persian.

G. Fill in the blanks using the words in the box:

تو ـ ایرانی ـ اسم ـ آزمایشگاه ـ
داری ـ دختر ـ چند ـ ساعت ـ شماره
فردا ـ چطور ـ کجا ـ اتاق

مینا: سلام مریم. حالت .... است؟

مریم: بد نیست، متشکرم .... چطوری؟

مینا: خوبم. تو ....کلاس انگلیسی ....؟

مریم: بله، ....هشت کلاس انگلیسی دارم.

مینا: کلاس انگلیسی ات.......... ست؟

مریم: نزدیک.......... زبان است.

مینا: کلاستان در اتاق.......... بیست است یا بیست و یک؟

مریم: در ....شماره بیست و یک است.

مینا: کلاس انگلیسی.......... تا دانشجو دارد؟

مریم: ده تا، شش تا پسر و چهار تا..........

مینا: استاد انگلیسی شما.......... است یا آمریکائی؟

مریم: آمریکائی است. ....ایشان خانم جانسون است.

H. Role-Play

Situation cards are designed to help the students initiate conversation. The English instructions on the cards are not to be translated into Persian; they are merely guidelines for generating meaningful dialogues in Persian about the specific situations indicated on the cards. This type of role-playing encourages students to ask as well as answer questions.

Situation Card # 1

You are meeting Sara in your class:

1. Greet her.
2. Ask her name.
3. Ask her where she is from, and what she is studying.
4. Ask if she knows Persian...
5. Find out what her native language is.

Situation Card # 2

You are meeting Robert in your Persian class:

1. Greet him.
2. Ask him how he is.
3. Ask him his Iranian friend's name.
4. Ask him if his friend is from Tehran.
5. Find out what his friend is studying at the university.
6. Ask him if he lives near the university.

I. Fill in the blanks with the independent form of the letters.

	۱
برای چه	۲
	۳
ل	۴
	۵
	۶
	۷

٤٠	۸
نام	۹
۷	۱۰
	۱۱
۵	۱۲
	۱۳

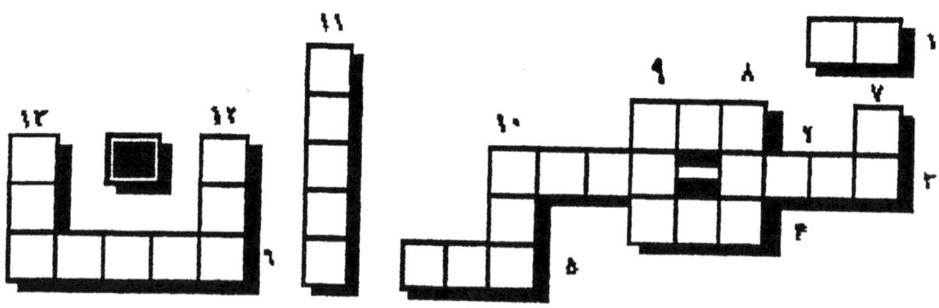

درس دوم

۱ـ گفتگو

برخورد و آشنائی

زبان و ملیّت

۲ـ خواندن

۳ـ یادداشتهای انگلیسی

تلفظ خ ـ ق

٤ـ دستور زبان

فعل بودن

جمله خبری، جمله پرسشی

نشانه را، زمان حال ساده

۵ـ تمرین و تکلیف

معنی انگلیسی	کلمه‌های تازه
excuse me	ببخشید
Mr.	آقا
Mrs. Miss	خانم
from where	کجایی
I am	هستم
you are	هستید
a little	کمی
Persian	فارسی
professor	استاد
Arabic	عربی
Egyptian	مصری
German	آلمانی
Turkish	ترکی
Hebrew	عبری
Russian	روسی
to live	زندگی کردن

گفتگو

برخورد و آشنائی

سینا	سلام خانم.
مریم	سلام آقا.
سینا	حالتان خوب است؟
مریم	مرسی. بد نیست.
سینا	ببخشید خانم، اسم شما چیست؟
مریم	اسم من مریم است.
سینا	شما دانشجو هستید؟
مریم	بله، من دانشجو هستم.
سینا	این آقا هم دانشجوست؟
مریم	بله، ایشان هم دانشجوست.
سینا	اسم ایشان چیست؟
مریم	پرویز است.
سینا	پرویز ایرانی است؟
مریم	آره، ایرانی است.

ملیّت

مینا آزادی

ایرانی

رابرت گرین

آمریکائی

کیمیکو ناشو

ژاپنی

نیکل ماسه

فرانسوی

مارک اشمیت

آلمانی

بنی کلارک

انگلیسی

زبان و ملیّت

نادر خانم شما کجائی هستید؟

باربارا من آمریکائی ام.

نادر فارسی می دانید؟

باربارا بله، کمی فارسی می دانم.

نادر استاد فارسی شما کجائی است؟

باربارا ایرانی است.

نادر استاد عربی کجائی است؟

باربارا ایشان مصری است.

نادر آن خانم عربی می داند؟

باربارا نخیر عربی نمی داند.

نادر فارسی می داند؟

باربارا بله، فارسی خوب می داند.

نادر انگلیسی چطور؟

باربارا انگلیسی هم می داند.

پُرسش:

۱ـ باربارا کجائی است؟

۲ـ ایشان فارسی می داند؟

۳ـ استاد فارسی باربارا کجائی است؟

٤ـ استاد عربی مصری است یا ایرانی؟

۵ـ دوست باربارا فارسی می داند یا عربی؟

Study the name of countries, languages and nationalities.

کِشور	زَبان	ملّیت
ایران	فارسی	ایرانی
افغانستان	دری ـ پشتو	افغانی
تاجیکستان	تاجیکی	تاجیک
پاکِستان	اُردو	پاکستانی
ترکیه	ترکی	ترک
عراق	عربی	عراقی
مِصر	عربی	مصری
آمریکا	انگلیسی	آمریکایی
فَرانسه	فرانسه	فرانسوی
آلمان	آلمانی	آلمانی
مکزیک	اسپانیولی	مکزیکی

خواندن

پرویز

مریم

این پسر ایرانی است. اسم او پرویز است.

من پرویز را می شناسم.

این دختر ایرانی است. اسم او مریم است.

ما مریم را می شناسیم.

پرسش:

اسم آن پسر چیست؟

اسم آن دختر چیست؟

کی مریم را می شناسد؟

می شناسم	می شناسیم
می شناسی	می شناسید
می شناسد	می شناسند

با نامهای پسران و دختران ایرانی آشنا شوید.

نام

لادن	پرویز
مینا	کوروش
نیلوفر	داریوش
لاله	انوشیروان
مریم	محّمد
لیلا	علی
زهرا	مهدی
بتول	حسین

خواندن

من یک دوست ایرانی دارم. اسم او احمد است. احمد دانشجوست، در این دانشگاه انگلیسی می خواند. من احمد را خوب می شناسم چون با او در یک خانه زندگی می کنم.

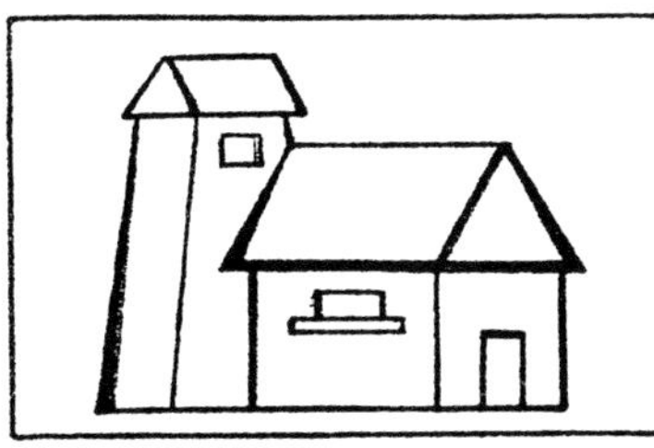

خانه

پرسش:

۱ـ اسم دوست شما چیست؟

۲ـ احمد در کدام دانشگاه انگلیسی می خواند؟

۳ـ کی احمد را خوب می شناسد؟

می خوانم	می خوانیم
می خوانی	می خوانید
می خواند	می خوانند

تمرین خواندن

۱ـ

نادر این خانم کجایی است؟

مینا ژاپنی است.

نادر اسم کوچک ایشان چیست؟

مینا کیمیکو است.

۲ـ

نادر این آقا هندی است یا چینی؟

مینا هندی است.

نادر نام خانوادگی ایشان چیست؟

مینا بوتو است.

۳ـ

نادر　ببخشید، آقای اپیکچی کجائی است؟

مینا　اهل آنکارا است.

نادر　اسم کوچک ایشان چیست؟

مینا　علی است.

٤ـ

نادر　شما خانم کلارک را می شناسید؟

مینا　بله، ایشان را خوب می شناسم.

نادر　خانم کلارک انگلیسی است؟

مینا　بله، انگلیسی است.

۵-

نادر اسم کوچک این خانم چیست؟

مینا نیکل است

نادر نیکل فرانسوی است یا آلمانی است؟

مینا فرانسوی است. اهل پاریس است.

٦-

نادر آقای اشمیت کجائی است؟

مینا ایشان آلمانی است، اهل مونیخ است.

نادر شما ایشان را می شناسید؟

مینا بله، ایشان را خوب می شناسم.

دوست برادرم است.

تلفظ خ

کلمه های زیر را بخوانید و به تلفظ خ توجه کنید.

خروس

۱

خوک

۲

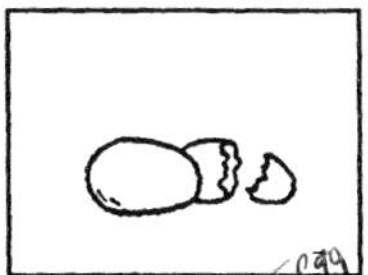

تخم مُرغ

۳

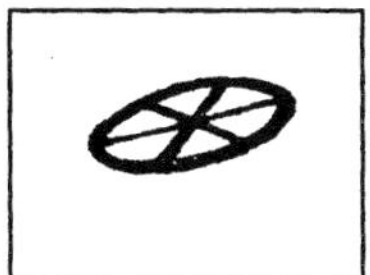

چرخ

۴

دوچرخه

۵

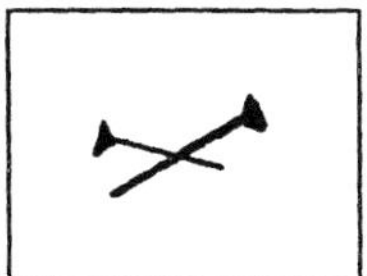

میخ

۶

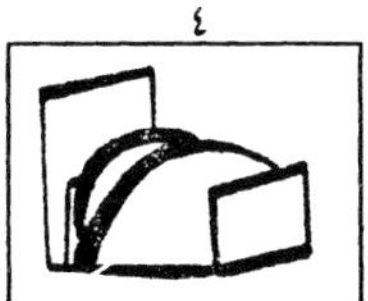

تختخواب

۷

خطر

۸

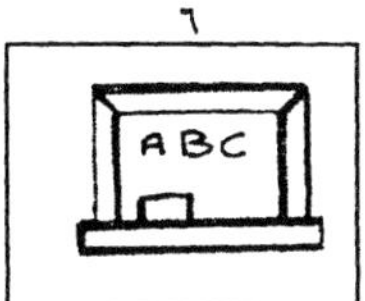

تخته سیاه

۹

در نامهای زیر به تلفظ (خ) توجه کنید

خاور

گلرخ

فخری

فرخنده

خسرو

بختیار

خدایار

The Consonant /q/ ق / غ

The consonant غ is produced like the consonant ق except that the passage of the air stream is continuous with an audible friction. In Tehrani dialect and speech of most educated Iranians, the two consonants are pronounced the same.

تلفظ ق/غ

به تلفظ کلمه های زیر گوش کنید و به تلفظ ق/غ توجه کنید.

قایق
۱

قطار
۲

مُرغابی
۳

قیچی
٤

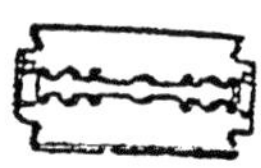
تیغ
۵

قاشق
٦

قلم
۷

قفل
۸

چراغ
۹

a. Listen to the tape and check the appropriate response

1 2 3 4 5

6 7 8 9 10

b. How many syllables do you identify in the expressions you hear on the tape?

1.--- 2.--- 3. --- 4. --- 5. --- 6. ---

7. --- 8. --- 9. --- 10. --- 11. --- 12. ---

c. Look at the pictures, then answer each of the questions you hear during the pause given.

یادداشت های انگلیسی

First Names in Persian

First names that Iranian parents adopt for their children fall in several patterns. The names can tell us about their parents' religious or ethnic affiliation and attitudes towards nationalism, folk beliefs, and socio-cultural characteristics as illustrated in the following categories.

- **Religious Names**

الف – نامهای دختران

۱– بتول ۲– زهرا ۳– مریم
۴– فاطمه ۵– لیلا ۶– خدیجه
۷– الهه ۸– آمنه ۹– معصومه

ب – نامهای پسران

۱– محمّد ۲– علی ۳– حسن
۴– حسین ۵– مهدی ۶– موسی
۷–کاظم ۸– رضا ۹– عبّاس

Compound names with علی, محمد, and الله. As well as some of their attributes and titles, is customary with religious names. For example.

۱– محمدحسن ۲– علی رضا ۳– عبدالله

The Use of The suffix ی and the Expression اهلِ

The stressed suffixed ی is a productive suffix in Persian that has a few meanings. When added to a place name or ethnic group it denotes a person's origin, e.g.,

آقای جمشیدِ تهرانی
خانم مینا بختیاری

The word اهل may also be used with a geographical name or an ethnic group to denote a person's origin, as in the examples below:

استاد انگلیسی مریم اهلِ نیویورک است.
دوست آمریکائی سارا اهلِ فلوریداست.

Note that the suffixation of the stressed ی to a place name of western origin, particularly with primary stress on non-final syllable, presents a pronunciation difficulty. The common practice is the use of اهلِ with western names, e.g.,

آقای نیکسون اهلِ کالیفرنیا و خانم ایشان
اهلِ واشنگتن است.
استاد انگلیسیِ ما اهل لندن است.

When the word اهل occurs to nouns and adjectives it may denote one who is endowed with or possesses of a specified quality, craft, belief, etc., e.g.,

writer(s)	اهلِ قلم
artist(s)	اهلِ هنر
learned men, the religious authrities	اهلِ علم
pleasure-seeking	اهلِ دِل
member(s) of the household	اهلِ خانه

Consonants with no Counterpart in English

As discussed earlier, most Persian counterparts are close enough to their English counterparts so that special description and practice is not necessary. These include the consonants /b/, /p/, /d/, /t/, /v/, /f/, /j/, /k/, /m/, /n/, /z/, /s/, /g/, /č/, /š/. Other consonants are basically like their English counterparts with slight differences, as discussed earlier in this textbook. These include the consonants /1/, /r/, and /h/.

A few consonants, however, present problems to speakers of English because they do not occur in English. Students often substitute the closest English sounds for the unfamiliar Persian sound. For example, the Persian /x/ is often replaced with a /k/ sound by English speakers. As a result, the word /xar/ "thorn" is pronounced /kar/ "work," which does not convey the speaker's meaning.

The consonant /x/ خ

In pronouncing this sound, you should place the back of the tongue against the velum, allowing the air stream to pass between the tongue and the velum. The articulation of /x/ is similar to a /k/ except that the point of articulation is further back in the mouth.

The contrast between /x/ and /k/ is observed in the following minimal pairs.

work	کار	thorn	خار
dark	تاریک	history	تاریخ

The consonant /q/ق

When making the Persian sound /q/, you will cause the flow of air to stop momentarily; thus, this sound is called a "stop". As you make this sound you will press the back of the tongue against the soft palate and uvula. The consonant /q/ occurs at the beginning, in the middle, and the end of words.

دستور زبان

The Verb To Be بودن

The verb بودن is different from all other verbs in Persian, and it is necessary to give this verb special treatment. The particular functions of the verb include the following:

- بودن has three stems other verbs have two stems - past and present. The three stems of 'to be' are هست 'present' بود 'past' and باش 'subjunctive'.

- بودن has two sets of forms, namely short and long forms, which may be used interchangeably.

- بودن may have a double function. It may be used as a linking verb, and as an auxiliary verb. As a linking verb it takes a complement, and as an auxiliary it is used in the formation of present and past perfect tenses.

- The negative prefix نَ is not used with the present tense. The negative stem نیست 'is not' is used with the verb endings to express negation.

* * *

Compare the following pairs of sentences containing the long and short forms of the verb 'to be'.

الف – خانم و آقای پرویزی تهرانی هستند.

ب – خانم و آقای پرویزی تهرانی اند.

الف – شما استاد هستید.

ب – شما استادید.

الف – ما حالا در کلاس هستیم.

ب – ما حالا در کلاسیم.

Short Forms (after consonants)	Long Forms
م	هستم
ی	هستی
-	است
یم	هستیم
ید	هستید
ند	هستند

In words ending in a vowel, the following spelling rules are observed.

- If the final vowel is /ā/ or /u/ , the semivowel ی is inserted.
- In words ending in the vowel sound /i/ or /e/ spelled with the letters ی and ه (hé) respectively, the letter الف is inserted.

دانایم.

دانائیم.

دانشجویم

دانشجوئیم.

ایرانی ام.

آمریکائی اید.

خسته اید.

خسته اند.

Pattern of Statements

Pattern 2: subject + intransitive verb

A verb that has no object is an intransitive verb. Predicate of intransitive verbs may have adverbs and prepositional phrases as illustrated in the examples below.

Predicate	Subject
دیروز صبح به کلاس آمد.	۱ - استاد فارسی ما
روی صندلی نشست.	۲ - پرویز
امروز به آزمایشگاه نرفت.	۳ - سارا
حالا به آزمایشگاه زبان می رویم.	۴ - من و نادر

Pattern 3: subject + direct object + transitive verb

In this pattern the direct object, which may be a noun, a pronoun, or a noun phrase is the receiver of the action. Predicates may have adverbs and prepositional phrases as in the following sentences.

Predicate	Subject
پرویز را خوب می شناسیم.	۱ - من و سارا
کتابش را روی میز گذاشت.	۲ - نادر
آن جمله را روی تخته سیاه نوشت.	۳ - استاد فارسی

Pattern 4: subject + direct object + indirect object + verb:

In this pattern there are two objects in the predicate. These two objects are called, in order, the direct object and the indirect object. If we omit the second object the pattern becomes pattern number 3, e.g.,

استاد ما آن جمله را روی تخته سیاه نوشت.

نادر کتابش را به من داد.

Note:

- if we omit the indirect object the pattern becomes a sentence of pattern 3.
- The indirect object is a often a prepositional phrase
- The indirect object may be defined as " the person or thing for whom or on whose behalf an action is carried out"
- A Short list of transitive verbs includes the following:

to give	دادن
to write	نوشتن
to say	گفتن
to ask	پرسیدن
to buy	خریدن
to sell	فروختن
to send	فرستادن
to beat	زدن
to kill	کشتن

- **"Yes/No" Questions**

"Yes/No" questions anticipate بله or نخیر for an answer, as the name suggests. Compare the following two sentences.

Statement شما فردا ساعت ده کلاس فارسی دارید.

Question شما فردا ساعت ده کلاس فارسی دارید؟

Notice that the words and the word order are exactly the same in both sentences. The only difference is the intonation: a direct statement has a falling intonation but the question has a rising intonation. If the sentences are spoken, the listener can tell that one is a statement and the other a question from the intonation.

- **"Or" Questions**

In an "or" question, there is a choice between two or more options. The Persian word for "or" is یا . Each sentence of this type is actually a combination of two basic sentence patterns, as illustrated in the following example:

این کتاب است یا دفتر است؟

شما فارسی می دانید یا عربی؟

سارا فرانسه می خواند یا انگلیسی؟

One variety of "or" question offers a choice between something and its negation by simply adding نه "no" at the end of the question, as in the following examples:

شما فردا صبح کلاس فارسی دارید یا نه؟

ما امروز بعد از ظهر آزمایشگاه زبان داریم یا نه؟

Question-Word Questions

As in English, Persian can introduce an interrogative sentence with a variety of "question words" with which the speaker asks for specified information signaled by the question words. The following are the most common "question words".

what	چه (چی)
who	کی (که)
when	کِی
where	کجا
which	کدام
how much/how many	چند
why	چرا
how	چطور
how	چگونه
how much	چقدر

Tag-Questions

As you can see, each tag question consists of two parts, a statement and a tag placed at the end of a sentence, thereby making that sentence into a yes/no question. The tag in Persian is invariable in form, whether the statement is affirmative or negative, the tense is present or past, the tag remains the same. Tag questions are used to elicit agreement to the first part of the sentence.

شما امروز ساعت ده کلاس فارسی دارید، اینطور نیست؟

سارا دیروز به آزمایشگاه زبان رفت ، اینطور نیست؟

ما فردا کلاس نداریم، اینطور نیست؟

The postposition را

As you notice in Patterns 3 and 4, in which the verbs are transitive, the direct objects are marked with the postposition را to indicate that definite and specific nouns are understood. e.g.,

ما امروزز درس دوم را خواندیم.

We studied lesson two today.

پرویز آن جمله را روی تخته سیاه نوشت.

Parviz wrote the sentence on the blackboard.

In contemporary Persian the postposition را must be used with inherently specific objects, therefore, with personal names and pronouns as in the examples below.

من سارا خوب می شناسم.

I know Sara well.

امروز صبح او را در کلاس دیدم

I saw her in the Persian class today.

There are, however, exceptions to this general statement. The postposition /ra/, for example, would not be used in sentences in which the following rules are in operation.

- •When suffixed pronouns are used as direct object the -postposition /ra/ is not used.

امروز صبح دیدمش.

I saw her in the morning.

- When a contrast is implied, studying Persian as opposed to other languages

ما فارسی می خوانیم نه عربی.

We study Persian not Arabic
(Persian as opposed to Arabic)

- C) The absence of /ra/ with a direct object may also signify indefiniteness of the object, and stands for a whole class of things as illustrated in the examples below.

من قهوه نمی خورم. چای لطف کنید.

I don't take coffee, give me tea, please.

من معمولاً بعد از شام کتاب می خوانم.

I usually read books after dinner.

- D) The use of /ra/ that indicates indefiniteness is more common with plural forms of the nouns, e.g.,

صادق هدایت، نویسنده معروف ایرانی، داستان های

جالب توجهی نوشته است.

Sadeq Hedayat, the famous Persian author, has written a lot of interesting stories

Other uses of the postposition /ra/, which are considered secondary in contemporary Persian, may be traced mainly in older form of the language. The following examples illustrate the point.

- **Indirect object را**

احمد را بگویید به من نامه بنویسد.

Tell Ahmad to write a letter to me.

- **Adverbial را**

تابستان را در ییلاق گذراندیم.

We spent the summer in the country side.

- **را substituting prepositions**

The following examples illustrate the use of /ra/ in the older form of the language.

گفتمش ما را چه آوردی.

(به او گفتم برای ما چه آوردی.)

I told her if she brought anything for us.

تو را به خدا !

For God's sake! (I swear to you by God.)

- **The possessive /ra/**

او را پسری است.

(او پسری دارد.)

He has a son.

- **The Spelling and Pronunciation of /ra/**

In written Persian /ra/ should not be joined to its preceding word. In a limited number of words, such as مرا 'me', چرا 'why', زیرا 'because' the postposition /ra/ is written joined to its preceding word. /ra/ is terminal, and can not be followed by other suffixes. In a noun phrase, /ra/ is added to the last word in the phrase. For example.

درس دوم فارسی را خواندیم.

In spoken Persian the particle is pronounced /o/ after a word that ends with a consonant, and /ro/ or /re/ after vowels. The postposition does not receive stress when it is pronounced with the preceding word.

The Simple Present Tense

It is formed from the prefix می the present stem of the verb, and the verb endings.

می + present stem + verb endings

می نویسیم We write

The verbs بودن and داشتن do not usually take the prefix می.

داریم We have

هستند They are

Uses of the Simple Present Tense

The simple present tense is used to express:

- habitual and repeated actions. This is the most common use of the tense.

For example:

من هر روز درس می خوانم.

I study every day.

- actions taking place at a given moment

حالا فارسی می خوانم.

I am studying Persian now.

- actions taking place in the future

فردا شما را می بینم.

I'll see you tomorrow.

تمرین و تکلیف

A. Fill in the (   ) with the number of the English equivalent.

1. college student	استاد	( )
2. professor	اهلِ	( )
3. university	دانشجو	( )
4. native of	فرانسوی	( )
5. France	مصری	( )
6. a Frenchman	فرانسه	( )
7. Arab	جمله	( )
8. coffee	دانشگاه	( )
9. Egyptian	عرب	( )
10. sentence	ببخشید	( )
11. blackboard	دانستن	( )
12. German	آلمانی	( )
13. excuse me	قهوه	( )
14. eyeglasses	تخته سیاه	( )
15. to know (something)	شناختن	( )
16. house	عینک	( )
17. language lab	خانه	( )
18. to know (somebody)	آزمایشگاه زبان	( )

B. Repeat the following sentences using the long forms of 'to be':

۱ـ من دانشجوی این مدرسه ام، فارسی می خوانم.

۲ـ مریم و نادر ایرانی اند، دردانشگاه میشیگان انگلیسی وکامپیوتر می خوانند.

۳ـ ما دانشجوئیم، در این کلاس فارسی می خوانیم.

٤ـ استادان فارسی ما ایرانی اند.

٥ـ استادان انگلیسی مریم و نادر آمریکائی اند.

٦ـ ایشان اهل میشیگان اند.

C. Repeat the following sentences using the short forms of 'to be':

۷ـ پرویز و مریم ایرانی هستند.

۸ـ شما کجائی هستید؟

۹ـ الیزابت و سارا هر دو دانشجوی رشته زبان شناسی هستند.

۱۰ـ ایشان حالا در آزمایشگاه زبان هستند.

۱۱ـ من بعد از ظهر تا ساعت دو در کتابخانه هستم.

۱۲ـ شما از دوستان پرویز بزرگتر هستید؟

D. Letters and sounds

How many letters and sounds do you identify in each word listed in the grid. Write the number of the letters and sounds as indicated below:

Column 1. Total number of letters
2. Total number of sounds.
3. Number of consonants.
4. Number of non-connectors.

		۱	۲	۳	۴
۱	استاد				
۲	فارسی				
۳	من				
۴	ایرانی				
۵	است				
۶	او				
۷	انگلیسی				
۸	و				
۹	فرانسه				
۱۰	می داند				
۱۱	اما				
۱۲	ایشان				
۱۳	آلمانی				
۱۴	نمی داند				

E. Match the pictures with nationalities listed in Persian.

اسپانیولی اسکاتلندی هندی چینی ویتنامی

روس عرب مصری مکزیکی

۱

۲

۳

٤

٥

٦

۷

۸

۹

F. Check بله or نخیر

Read the following sentences and check under 'yes' or 'no'.

		بله نخیر
		بله نخیر
۱	ایران در آسیاست.	
۲	افعانستان و پاکستان هم در آسیاست؟	
۳	قاهره پایتخت مصر است.	
۴	کوبا در آمریکای شمالی است؟	
۵	کانادا هم در آمریکای شمالی است؟	
۶	استرالیا و نیوزیلند در اقیانوسیه است؟	
۷	پایتخت آمریکا شهر واشنگتن است؟	
۸	مکزیک هم در آمریکای شمالی است؟	
۹	فرانسه در اروپاست.	
۱۰	آلمال و اسپانیا هم در اروپاست؟	

G. Persian Word Hunt

Directions: Decide on the correct Persian translations for the English words listed below. Then circle the words in the puzzle. Note that Persian words are spelled from right to left.

Persian	Miss	hello	yes	please	good	favor
English	Mister	good-bye	no	thank you	bad	name

۱۳	۱۲	۱۱	۱۰	۹	۸	۷	٦	۵	٤	۳	۲	۱	
ه	ذ	ش	م	ک	ی	س	ی	ل	گ	ن	ا	ف	۱
ژ	گ	ژ	ت	م	ز	ک	ط	ظ	ط	ر	ا	ه	۲
ف	د	ق	ش	ه	م	س	ک	خ	ح	ر	س	ن	۳
ه	ک	ز	ک	ه	ک	د	ض	ح	س	ن	س	خ	٤
ظ	خ	ش	ر	ض	گ	ر	ل	ی	س	ن	ل	ی	۵
ب	و	خ	م	ا	ل	س	چ	ن	و	ح	خ	ر	٦
گ	ص	د	س	س	غ	ت	گ	د	ب	ه	س	گ	۷
ذ	ک	ا	ذ	م	ک	ش	س	ه	ر	ق	ف	ذ	۸
ف	م	ح	ش	گ	د	ض	ح	ح	ف	خ	ظ	ش	۹
ذ	ظ	ا	ق	آ	و	و	س	ع	غ	ا	ر	ص	۱۰
ق	ک	ف	ه	گ	س	ه	ل	ب	م	ن	ک	گ	۱۱
ق	ف	ظ	ژ	غ	ض	ش	ط	گ	ذ	م	ز	ز	۱۲
ح	د	ی	ی	ا	م	ر	ف	ب	ص	خ	ن	چ	۱۳

H. Questions and Answers

Check a, b, c, or d that corresponds to each question.

1. The independent form of the letter is used when:

   a. the letter is connected only to a following letter
   b. the letter is connected only to a preceding letter
   c. the letter is connected to a preceding and to a following letter
   d. the letter is not connected to any letter, preceding or following

2. The initial form of the letter is used when:

   a. the letter is connected only to a following letter
   b. the letter is connected only to a preceding letter
   c. the letter is connected to a preceding and to a following letter
   d. the letter is not connected to any letter, preceding or following

3. The medial form of the letter is used when:

   a. the letter is connected only to a following letter
   b. the letter is connected only to a preceding letter
   c. the letter is connected to a preceding and to a following letter
   d. the letter is not connected to any letter, preceding or following

4. The final form of the letter is used when:

   a. the letter is connected only to a following letter
   b. the letter is connected only to a preceding letter
   c. the letter is connected to a preceding and to a following letter
   d. the letter is not connected to any letter, preceding or following

5. How many dots can a Persian letter have?

   a. one b. two c. three d. one, two or three

6. How many forms does a non-connector have?

   a. Independent and final forms
   b. Independent, medial, and final forms
   c. Initial, medial and final forms
   d. Independent, initial, medial, and final forms.

7. A connector letter:

   a. always connects to the letter that comes before it.
   b. always connects to the letter that comes after it.
   c. doesn't have an initial or medial form.
   d. all of the above.

8. A non-connector letter:

   a. sometimes connects to the letter before it.
   b. never connects to the letter after it.
   c. doesn't have an initial or medial form.
   d. all of the above.

9. How many variants can a Persian letter have?

   a. only one b. two or three c. four d. only two

10. How many letters does the Persian alphabet have?

   a. 26 b. 28 c. 32 d. 36

11. Persian words and numerals are written in which direction?

   a. Words and numerals from left to right.
   b. Words from left to right; numerals from right to left.
   c. Words from right to left; numerals from left to right.
   d. Words and numerals from right to left.

12. Which forms do connector letters have?

   a. Independent and final forms.
   b. Independent, medial, and final forms.
   c. Initial, medial, and final forms.
   d. Independent, initial, medial and final forms.

نقشه استان مازندران

این شهر ها را روی نقشه مازندران پیدا کنید.

۱ـ ساری (مرکز استان)

۲ـ رامسر

۳ـ بابل

٤ـ بابلسر

٥ـ نوشهر

٦ـ بهشهر

۷ـ آمل

۸ـ کلاردشت

جدول

خانه های جدول را پر کنید

از بالا به پایین

۱ـ خالی نیست.

۲ـ یکی از حرفهای اضافه است.

۳ـ با آن راه می رویم.

۴ـ نام دریاچه ای است در آذربایجان غربی.

۵ـ با آن می شنویم.

۶ـ

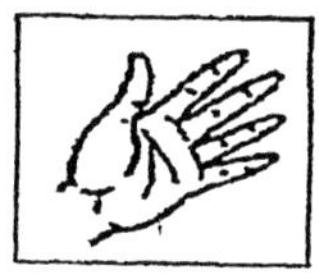

۷ـ

از راست به چپ

۸ـ

۹ـ آن را می خوانیم.

۱۰ـ آب بازی

۱۱.

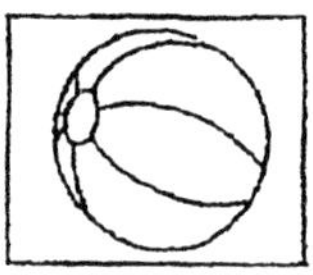

۱۲ـ نزدیک نیست.

۱۳ـ بی سیم.

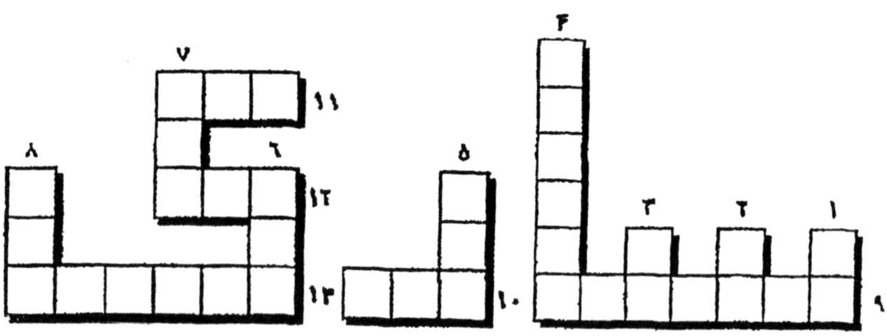

درس سوم

۱ـ گفتگو

ساعت چند است؟

درخواست و تقاضا

۲ـ خواندن

۳ـ یادداشتهای انگلیسی

تلفظ ل ر ه

۴ـ دستور زبان

نشانه های جمع

اضافه

جمله امری

۵ـ تمرین و تکلیف

کلمه‌های تازه	معنی انگلیسی
دقیقه	minute
ثانیه	second
نیم	half
ربع	quarter
درست	right, correct
حالا	now
روز	day
دیروز	yesterday
تعطیل	holiday, off
لطفاً	kindly, please
به	to
هفته	week
بسته	closed
دادن(ده)	to give
بفرمائید	here you are, please
کلمه	word

ساعت رو میزی

ساعت دیواری

ساعت مچی

ساعت چند است؟

نادر راستی، تو فردا کلاس فارسی داری؟

سارا آره، ساعت نه کلاس دارم.

نادر امروز ساعت چند کلاس داری؟

سارا امروز کلاس ندارم. یک ساعت آزمایشگاه زبان دارم.

نادر ساعت چند آزمایشگاه داری؟

سارا ساعت ده.

نادر حالا به ساعت تو نه و نیم است؟

سارا نخیر نه و ربع است. به ساعت تو چند است؟

نادر نه و بیست دقیقه است.

سارا تو هم امروز آزمایشگاه زبان داری؟

نادر بله.

سارا ساعت چند آزمایشگاه داری؟

نادر ساعت یازده.

گفتگو

روزهای هفته

مینا	پرویز، امروز چند شنبه است؟
پرویز	دوشنبه است.
مینا	فردا چند شنبه است؟
پرویز	سه شنبه است.
مینا	دیروز یکشنبه بود؟
پرویز	بله، یکشنبه بود.
مینا	یکشنبه دانشگاه تعطیل است؟
پرویز	بله، یکشنبه دانشگاه تعطیل است.
مینا	راستی امروز نوزدهم است یا بیستم است؟
پرویز	بیستم است.
مینا	جمعه بیست و پنجم است؟
پرویز	نخیر، بیست و چهارم است.

اعداد زیر را بخوانید.

۵۰	٤۰	۳۰	۲۰	۱۰
۱۰۰	۹۰	۸۰	۷۰	٦۰
ده	بیست	سی	چهل	پنجاه
شصت	هفتاد	هشتاد	نود	صد

یادداشتهای انگلیسی

Days of the Week

◄

جمعه	پنج شنبه	چهارشنبه	سه شنبه	دوشنبه	یکشنبه	شنبه

In Iran, the first day of the week is Saturday شنبه beginning at sunset on Friday. جمعه is the Muslim Sabbath and is the day of worship when they assemble in mosques.

A week is هفته from هفت 'seven' and a day is twenty-four hours. The Arabic word جمعه replaced the Persian word آدینه. The day begins with the setting of the sun, so that when one says شب جمعه (literally: the night of Friday), for example, he means the night preceding Friday, that is Thursday evening. However, the expression جمعه شب means Friday night.

The Iranian Calendar

Two calendars, a solar calendar and a lunar calendar, are used in Iran. The هجری شمسی (Hegira Solar Calendar) is Iran's official calendar, which is used to mark national holidays and the beginning of the New Year. The year begins at the vernal equinox تحویل سال on the first day of spring which usually falls on the 1st day of فروردین Iranian New Year's Day coincides with March 20th or 21st.

Like the calendar used in Europe and America, it has 365 days and a leap year. The first six months have 31 days each and the following five months have 30 days each, and the twelfth month اسفند has 29 days except on a leap year when it has 30 days.

The two calendars have the same origin. Year one for both solar and lunar calendars begins in the year 622 A.D. with the migration of the Prophet Muhammad from Mecca to Medina.

The solar year 1379 + 621 = 2000 A.D

درخواست و تقاضا

(۱)

آقای وفائی، لطفاً کتابتان را باز کنید.

بسیار خوب

حالا لطفاً کتابتان را ببندید.

بسیار خوب.

آقای وفائی، لطفاً در کلاس را باز کنید.

خیلی خوب.

حالا لطفاً در را ببندید.

بسیار خوب

علی، کی در را بست؟

آقای وفائی در را بست.

حالا در کلاس باز است یا بسته است؟

بسته است.

در باز است

(۲)

فیروز خانم تهرانی، لطفاً گچ را به من بدهید.

خانم تهرانی بفرمائید.

فیروز من حالا چند کلمه روی تخته سیاه می نویسم.

۱

الف ـ پنجره را باز کن!

ب ـ لطفاً پنجره را باز کنید!

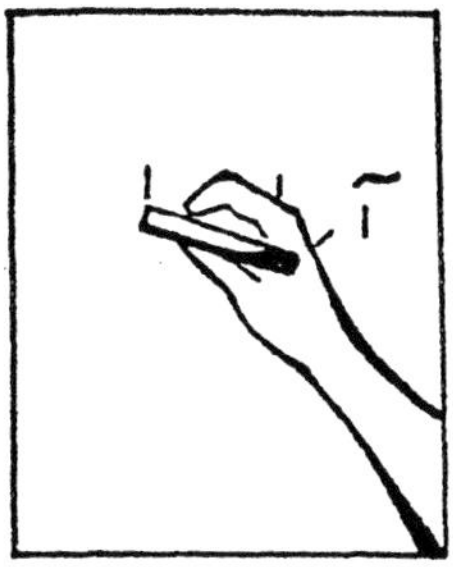

۲

الف ـ اسمت را بنویس!

ب ـ لطفاً اسمتان را بنویسید!

۳

الف ـ کتابت را باز کن!

ب ـ لطفاً کتابتان را باز کنید!

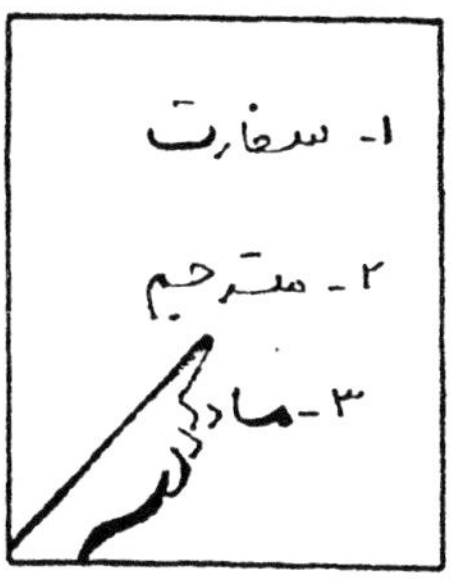

٤

الف ـ این کلمه ها را بخوان!

ب ـ لطفاً این کلمه ها را بخوانید!

کلمه‌های تازه	معنی انگلیسی
هفته	week ....
مردم....................	people...............
معمولاً....................	usually.............
آخر	end..................
یعنی....................	it means ....
استراحت کردن......	to take a rest .
اینطور....................	like this ....
مدرسه....................	school ....
اداره	office.............
فقط....................	only..............
بعضی....................	some.............
شهر....................	city................
بازار....................	market ....
حتّی....................	even ....
باز....................	open ....
غالباً....................	mostly.........
بعد از ظهر...........	aftenoon ....
کار کردن.............	to work .....

خواندن

روزهای هفته

یک هفته هفت روز است: شنبه، یکشنبه، دوشنبه، سه شنبه، چهارشنبه، پنج شنبه، جمعه. در آمریکا و اروپا مردم معمولاً هفته ای پنج روز کار می کنند و روزهای آخر هفته، یعنی شنبه و یکشنبه استراحت می کنند.

در ایران اینطور نیست. مدارس ادارات و بانک ها فقط روزهای جمعه تعطیل است. در بعضی شهرها، بازارها و بانک ها حتّی صبح جمعه هم باز است، ولی غالباً بعد از ظهر جمعه کسی کار نمی کند.

پرسش:

۱ـ یک هفته چند روز است؟

۲ـ در ایران روز اوّل هفته کدام است؟

۳ـ در آمریکا روز اوّل هفته کدام است؟

٤ـ در ایران مردم هفته ای چند روز کار می کنند؟

٥ـ در آمریکا مردم هفته ای چند روز کار می کنند؟

٦ـ در ایران چه روزی مدارس تعطیل است؟

ماههای سال

الف – بهار

۱– فروردین
۲– اردیبهشت
۳– خرداد

ب – تابستان

۴– تیر
۵– مرداد
۶– شهریور

ج – پائیز

۷– مهر
۸– آبان
۹– آذر

د – زمستان

۱۰– دی
۱۱– بهمن
۱۲– اسفند

هریک از ماههای بهار و تابستان سی و یک روز است. هریک از ماههای پائیز و زمستان سی روز است. ماه اسفند بیست و نه روز است و هر چهار سال یک مرتبه که سال کبیسه است سی روز می شود.

از
مثلهای فارسی

۱ـ دوستی دوستی آرد.

۲ـ هزار دوست کم است و یک دشمن بسیار.

۳ـ دوستی با مردم دانا نیکوست.

1. Friendship brings friendship .
2. A thousand friends are few, one enemy is too many.
3. It is advisable to make friends with learned people.

وقت طلاست

نگاهی به تقویم ایرانی

فروردین		ذیقعده ۱۴۱۸		March 1998
شنبه	۱	۲۲	آغاز سال ۱۳۷۷ خورشیدی	21
یکشنبه	۲	۲۳		22
دوشنبه	۳	۲۴		23
سه‌شنبه	۴	۲۵		24
چهارشنبه	۵	۲۶		25
پنجشنبه	۶	۲۷		26
جمعه	۷	۲۸		27

آغاز سال : ۱۳۸۴
ساعت ۱۶ و ۳ دقیقه و ۱۴ثانیه
روز شنبه ۳۰ اسفند
۱۳۸۳ خورشیدی

قرن بیست و یکم میلادی مطابق
قرن چهاردهم هجری خورشیدی

Pronunciation Practice تلفّظ ر

Listen to and repeat the following words. Pay particular attention to the pronunciation of the consonant /r/.

رادیو

۱

روزنامه

۲

رقص

۳

چرخ

٤

بَرگ

۵

ایران

٦

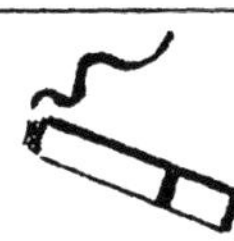

سیگار

۷

انگور

۸

چتر

۹

تلفّظ ل

Pronunciation Practice

Listen to and repeat the following words. Pay particular attention to the pronunciation of the consonant /1/.

لامپ

۱

لب

۲

لیوان

۳

لیمو

٤

گلابی

٥

گیلاس

٦

گل

۷

چنگال

۸

قفل

۹

Pronunciation Practice

تلفّظ ۵

Listen to and repeat the following words. Pay particular attention to the pronunciation of the consonant /h/.

هَویج

۱

هلو

۲

هندوانه

۳

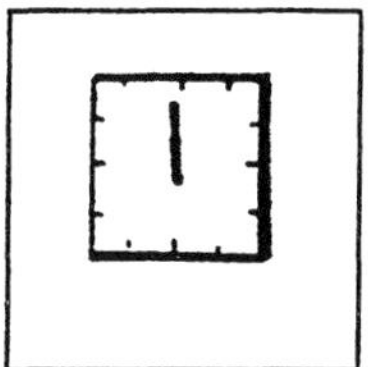

ظهر

٤

قهوه

۵

مهندس

٦

۱۴

چهارده

۷

ماه

۸

کلاه

۹

دستور زبان

The Plural Suffixes

A singular noun can be made plural by adding one of the plural suffixes. The most common plural suffixes are ها and آن

- ها is used for both animate and inanimate nouns as in the following examples.

Animate nouns:

دخترها	دختران	دختر
پسرها	پسران	پسر
مردها	مردان	مرد
زنها	زنان	زن

Inanimate nouns

مدادها مداد

میزها میز

- Certain parts of the body in pairs are also formed their plural with ان

چشمان چشم

ابروان ابرو

مژگان مژه

The plural forms of Arabic words used in Persian follow the rules mentioned above plus the following:

- ات is used with Arabic, Turkish and some Persian words, e.g.,

کلمات
words

ایلات
tribes

دهات
villages

- جات is used when the singular noun ends in a vowel, e.g.,

سبزیجات
vegetables

میوه جات
fruits

دستجات
groups

- ین in words of Arabic origin, e.g.,

معلّمین
teachers

مورّخین
historians

- ون joined to nouns ending in ی , e.g.,

ملّیون
nationalists

انقلابیون
revolutionaries

Spelling and Pronouncing Plurals

- Persian and Arabic plural suffixes are often written joined to the singular.

- The plural suffix ها is not joined to the singular in the following environment.

- In words that end with the vowel /e/. e.g.,

نامه ← نامه ها
letters

خانه ← خانه ها
houses

گوشه ← گوشه ها
corners

بچه ← بچه ها
children

Note that the above rule does not apply when the final letter ه represents the consonant /h/, e.g.,

ماهها
months

دانشگاهها
universities

کوهها
mountains

فروشگاهها
department stores

فرودگاهها
airports

- When the plural nouns denote certain types of people, e.g.,

  ایرانیان به شاعران بزرگ خود چون فردوسی ها،

  خیّام ها، سعدی ها، و حافظ ها افتخار می کنند.

  Iranians are proud of their great poets, such as Ferdowsi, Khayyam, Sa'di, and Hafez.

- When the suffix ان is added to the singular words ending in the vowel /e/, the final letter ه is replaced by the consonant گ as in the following words:

  بنده ← بندگان
  slaves

  گرسنه ← گرسنگان
  hungry ones

  تشنه ← تشنگان
  thirsty ones

  زنده ← زندگان
  living ones

  مرده ← مردگان
  dead ones

- In spoken Persian, the suffix ها is pronounced /a/ after consonants.
- If the singular word ends in the vowels /ā/ or /u/, the semivowel ی is inserted before the suffix ان . For example:

  دانشجویان
  college students

  آقایان
  gentlemen

- The final vowel /e/ of the singular word, in some cases is dropped before the Arabic suffix ات.

کلمه ← کلمات
words

جمله ← جملات
sentences

اداره ← ادارات
offices

- The plural suffix ان is not used with animate nouns borrowed from Western languages. The suffix ها is used with these words, e.g.,

دکترها
doctors

آرتیست ها
artists

دموکراتها
democrats

- When the subject in a sentence is an animate noun, the verb must agree with it in number, e.g.,

استاد انگلیسی ما آمریکائی است.

استادان انگلیسی ما آمریکائی هستند.

- When the subject is a plural inanimate noun, the verb is often used in singular e.g.,

کتاب روی میز است.

The book is on the table.

کتابها روی میز است.

The books are on the table.

کار برد اضافه در عبارات اسمی

The Connective /e/ اضافه

Study the following noun phrases in which اضافه connects nouns and their modifiers:

دوستِ ما
our friend

ساعتِ یازده
11:00 a.m.

استادِ عربی
the Arabic professor

دانشجویِ ایرانی
the Iranian student

درسِ چهارم
the fourth lesson

یکِ بعدازظهر
1:00 p.m.

آقایِ نادر تهرانی
Mr. Nader Tehrani

کتِ قهوه ای
the brown coat

اتاقِ کوچک
the small room

هوایِ گرم

the warm weather

پرچمِ ایران

the flag of Iran

آقای ایرانی

Mr. Irani

In the above examples, modified nouns are connected to their modifiers with اضافه - the connective /e/. Note that a modifier can be an adjective or another noun. When a noun ends with a vowel, the semivowel ی is inserted between the noun and the connective /e/ as in the following examples.

پای من

my foot

بازوی او

his arm

A noun may be modified with more than one modifier. An attribute of quality is placed immediately after the head noun and with the possessive thereafter as in the following examples.

مادر مهربان من

my kind mother

دانشجویان پرکار کلاس فارسی ما

The hard-working students of our Persian class

Notice that independent and suffixed pronouns are always placed at the end of the noun phrase, e.g.,

استاد زبان فارسی ما

our Persian language professor

دوست آمریکائی برادرتان

your brother's American friend

The Meanings of the Connective /e/

In general, the connective /e/ is used to modify, qualify or describe the head noun in a noun phrase. The following noun phrases illustrate the various meanings associated with the connective /e/.

#	***Meanings***	***Persian Examples***
1	possession	آپارتمان برادرم اتومبیل نو شما
2	material	کت چرمی اتاقک چوبی
3	naming	آقای پرویز کیانی خانم مریم امامی
4	time	ساعت ده صبح جمعه آینده
5	geographical origin	قالی ایران اتومبیل آلمانی
6	profession	رستم پهلوان حسنک وزیر
7	content	لیوان آبخوری قوری چای
8	action	تحصیلِ دانش فریفته هنر
9	metaphor	دست روزگار چهره گیتی

Imperative Sentences

Note the difference in verb form between the affirmative statements and the affirmative command.

شما فارسی می خوانید.

You study Persian.

فارسی بخوانید.

Study Persian!

The verbal prefix /mi/ is replaced by /be/, and the expressed subject شما is omitted in the imperative sentences. The verbal ending /id/ remains the same for both affirmative and the imperative sentences.

Negative Commands

In negative commands, the negative prefix /nā /replaces the prefix /be/ as in the following examples.

در را ببندید!

Close the door.

در را نبندید.

Don't close the door.

In formal/polite style, the second plural ending /id/ is used for the second person singular. However, no verb ending is used in the familiar singular as in the following:

پنجره را ببندید!

Close the window! (singular and plural)

پنجره را ببند!

Close the window (singular)

تمرین و تکلیف

A. Flags, Symbols and Countries

Which countries do the following flags and symbols of nations remind you of? Write down the name of the countries in the boxes.

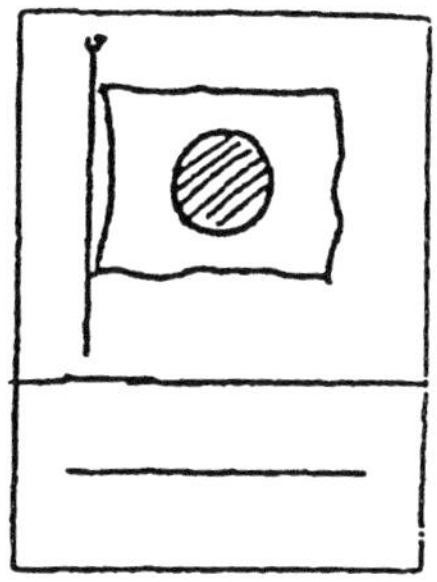

١

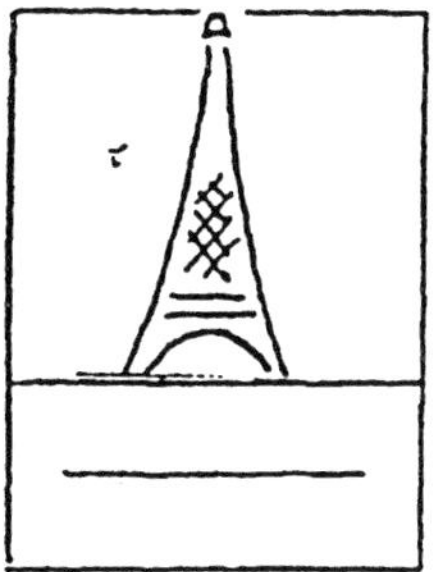

٢

٣

٤

٥

٦

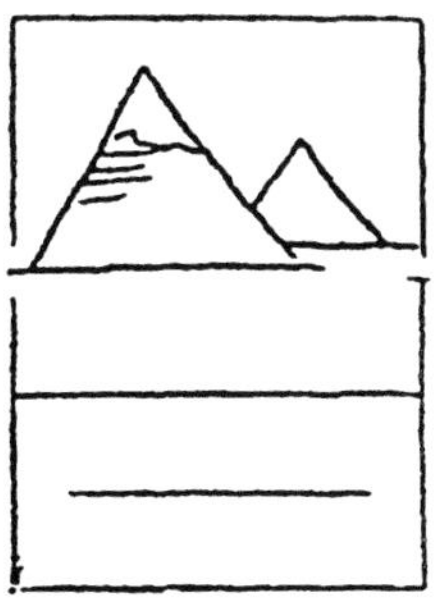

٧

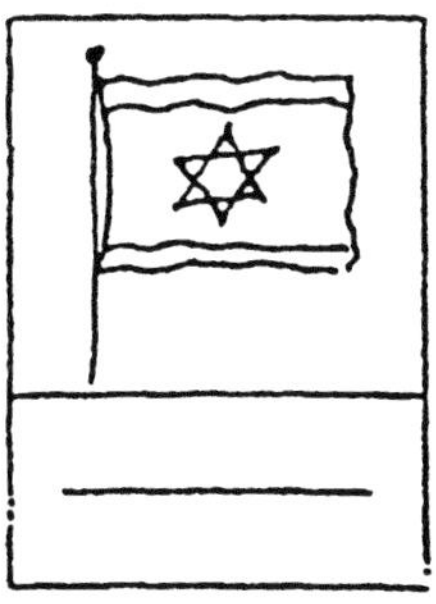

٨

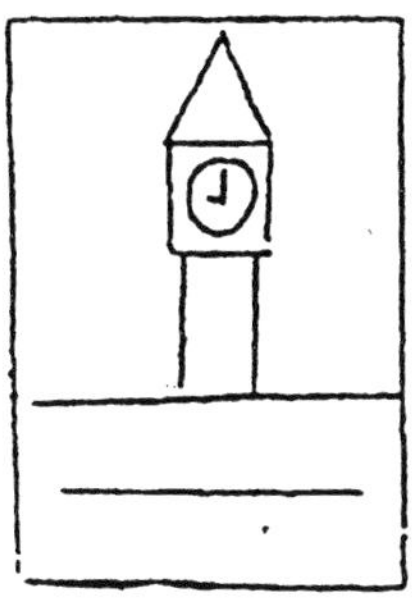

٩

B. Discourse Questionnaire

Try to guess the appropriate Persian response according to the situation.

1. When introducing yourself to someone you don't know, you might say:

الف – اسم من .... است.

ب – شما آمریکائی هستید؟

ج – اسم شما چیست؟

2. When your friend says خداحافظ, what would you say in response?

الف – متشکرم.

ب – بسلامت.

ج – بسیار خوب.

3. If your instructor gives you instructions in Persian that you don't understand, you would say:

الف – استاد، نمی دانم.

ب – لطفاً تکرار کنید.

ج – نخیر، نفهمیدم.

4. When you ask your younger brother to close the window, you might say:

الف – پنجره باز نیست بسته است.

ب – پرویز، پنجره را ببند!

ج – در و پنجره را ببندید.

5. When you offer someone a seat, you say:

الف – خیلی خوب

ب – بفرمائید.

ج – ببخشید.

6. If your friend uses a Persian word you don't know, you might politely ask:

الف – ببخشید، این کلمه یعنی چه؟

ب – راستی نمیدانم.

ج – بسیار خوب.

7. When someone compliments your fluency in Persian, you might say:

الف – ببخشید فارسی ام خوب نیست.

ب – لطفاً تکرار کنید.

ج – از لطف شما متشکرم.

8. 8. When you ask Miss Mina Tehrani to go to the board, you might say:

الف – مینا بیا پای تخته.

ب– خانم تهرانی، بیا پای تخته.

ج – خانم تهرانی، لطفاً بفرمائید پای تخته.

9. When introducing a classmate to your parents, you might say:

لف– مریم همکلاس من است. ایشان انگلیسی و تاریخ می خواند.

ب– ما فارسی و انگلیسی می خوانیم.

ج – استاد ما آمریکائی است.

C. Request Forms of the Verbs

Fill in the blanks with appropriate request forms of the verbs. Use the Persian equivalent of the verbs listed below.

1. close	6. come	11. talk
2. open	7. write	12. call up
3. read	8. give	13. sit down
4. repeat	9. don't go	14. stand up
5. give	10. be	15. don't translate

۱ـ خواهش می کنم در کلاس را ....

۲ـ حالا کتابتان را ....

۳ـ لطفاً درس، سوّم را..

٤ـ حالا این جمله ها را بعد از من ....

۵ـ کتابتان را به من..

٦ـ .... پای تخته.

۷ـ لطفاً اسمتان را به فارسی روی تخته..............................

۸ـ حالا گچ را به من ....

۹ـ امروز ساعت ده به آزمایشگاه زبان..............................

۱۰ـ ساعت یازده اینجا..

۱۱ـ لطفاً فارسی حرف..

۱۲ـ خواهش می کنم امشب به من تلفن................................

۱۳ـ لطفاً روی این صندلی..

١٤ـ ....اینجا.

D. Formal/Informal Requests

How do you say the following sentences in the formal style? Use appropriate titles of address with family names in the formal sentences.

informal	نادر کتابت را باز کن.	الف
		ب
informal	نادر این کلمه ها را بخوان.	الف
		ب
informal	نادر کتابت را به من بده.	الف
		ب
informal	نادر اسمت را روی تخته سیاه بنویس.	الف
		ب
informal	مینا بیا پای تخته.	الف
		ب
informal	مینا اسمت را به فارسی بنویس.	الف
		ب
informal	مینا این کلمه ها را بنویس.	الف
		ب
informal	مینا حالا گچ را به من بده.	الف
		ب
informal	درس چهارم را بخوان.	الف
		ب

E. Matching Pictures with the Words

Underline one of the words that matches the picture.

	تلویزیون	میز	رادیو	صندلی
	قفل	کیف	عینک	کتاب
	کلید	کاغذ	گچ	قلم
	چشم	دفتر	ساعت	عینک
	پنجره	تخته سیاه	در	دیوار
	نقشه	تلویزیون	تلفن	رادیو
	لیوان	گلابی	کلاه	گل

F. Combine each set of words into a noun phrase.

Example:

فارسی ‒ ‒ ما ‒ ‒ کلاس کلاس فارسی ما

۱ـ بیست ـ اتاق ـ شماره

....

۲ـ تاریخ ـ ایران ـ کلاس ـ ایشان

....

۳ـ ایرانی ـ دانشجو

....

٤ـ من ـ ایرانی ـ دوست

....

۵ـ کلاس ـ آمریکا ـ تاریخ

....

٦ـ یازده ـ اتاق ـ شماره

....

۷ـ برادر ـ شما ـ بزرگ

....

۸ـ کوچک ـ خواهر ـ مریم

....

۹ـ انگلیسی ـ ما ـ استاد

....

۱۰ـ بعد ـ هفت ـ ظهر ـ از

....

۱۱ـ اوّل ـ هفته ـ روز

....

۱۲ـ آخر ـ هفته ـ روز

....

۱۳ـ به ـ ربع ـ یک ـ هشت

....

۱٤ـ دقیقه ـ بیست ـ دوازده ـ به

....

۱۵ـ برادر ـ من ـ ایرانی ـ دوست

....

۱٦ـ فارسی ـ ایشان ـ استاد

....

۱۷ـ مادری ـ ما ـ زبان

....

Situation Card #3

You meet a girl in your Persian class.

1. Introduce yourself to her.
2. Ask her name and nationality.
3. Find out:

a. What foreign languages she knows and how well she speaks them.
b. How long she has studied Persian, why she is taking Persian, and whether she finds it an easy or difficult language.
c. If she is planning to take Persian next year.
d. If she has an opportunity to practice Persian with her Iranian friends.

Situation Card #4

You meet Reza, your Iranian friend, at the university restaurant.

1. Say hello to him.
2. Ask him how he is doing.
3. Offer him a seat.

While sitting at a table:

a. Ask him why he was not in class yesterday.
b. Find out if he will be in class next Monday.
c. Tell him you are looking forward to seeing him then.
d. Offer him a cup of coffee.
e. Remind him that an Iranian student has been invited to visit the Persian class next Monday.

When you have finished, say goodbye.

جدول

خانه های جدول را پر کنید.

از راست به چپ

۱ـ باز و بسته می شود.

۲ـ دریاچه ای است در آذربایجان غربی.

۳ـ زبان مردم ترکیه

٤ـ نزدیک نیست.

٥ـ یک نوع هواپیماست.

٦ـ آن را به نشانه سلامتی روی سفره هفت سین می گذارند.

از بالا به پائین

۷ـ محل

۸ـ اندک

۹ـ کشوری است در جنوب شرقی آسیا.

۱۰ـ آن را می پوشیم.

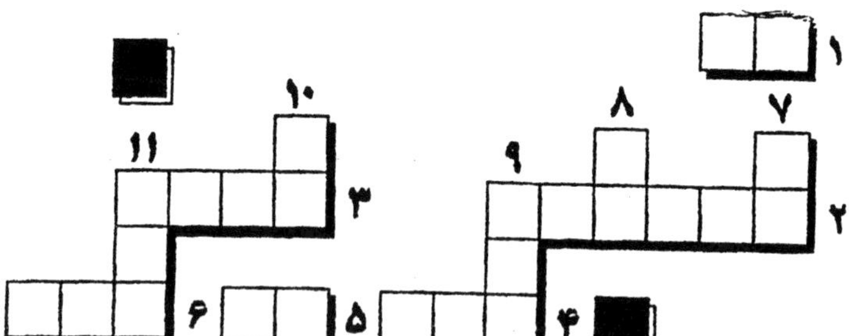

درس چهارم

۱ـ گفتگو

خانواده

کلاس فارسی

۲ـ خواندن

۳ـ یادداشتهای انگلیسی

۴ـ دستور زبان

حرف اضافه، زمان گذشته

فعل مرکب

عربی در فارسی، جمله تعجبی

۵ـ تمرین و تکلیف

معنی انگلیسی	کلمه‌های تازه
father	پدر ....
mother	مادر....................
brother	برادر....................
sister	خواهر..................
uncle	عمو.....................
uncle	دائی.....................
aunt.........................	خاله ....
aunt	عمّه....................
husband	شو هر (همسر)..
wife	زن (همسر).......
relative	خویشاوند..........
elementary school	دبستان.................
high school	دبیرستان.............
to begin	شروع کردن...........
to end....................	تمام کردن.............
building................	ساختمان..............
literature	ادبیّات..................
story	طبقه......................

گفتگو

خانواده

نادر ببخشید خانم، شما چند تا برادر دارید؟

مینا من یک برادر دارم.

نادر اسم برادرتان چیست؟

مینا اسمش مسعود است.

نادر مسعود از شما بزرگتر است یا کوچکتر است؟

مینا سه سال از من کوچکتر است.

نادر برادرتان به دبستان می رود؟

مینا نخیر به دبیرستان می رود، کلاس نهم است.

نادر شما خواهر هم دارید؟

مینا بله، دو تا خواهر دارم.

نادر خواهرهایتان از شما کوچکترند؟

مینا	خیر از من بزرگترند.
نادر	خواهرهایتان چکار می کنند؟
مینا	یک خواهرم دانشجوست، یکی هم با شوهرش در ایران زندگی می کند.

پرسش:

۱ـ مینا چند تا برادر دارد؟

۲ـ اسم برادر مینا چیست؟

۳ـ مسعود از مینا بزرگتر است یا کوچکتر است؟

٤ـ مینا چند سال از برادرش بزرگتر است؟

۵ـ مسعود دانش آموز دبیرستان است؟

٦ـ مسعود کلاس چندم است؟

۷ـ مینا چند تا خواهر دارد؟

۸ـ یکی از خواهرهایش دانشجوست؟

۹ـ خواهر مینا و شوهرش کجا زندگی می کنند؟

Additional questions:

۱۰ـ شما چند تا برادر دارید؟

۱۱ـ چند تا خواهر دارید؟

۱۲ـ دوست ایرانی تان در این شهر زندگی می کند؟

۱۳ـ پدر و مادرش در ایران زندگی می کنند؟

١٤ـ شما از دوست ایرانی تان بزرگترید؟

خویشاوندان مادری

پدر بزرگ ↔ مادر بزرگ

مادر — دائی ↔ زن دائی — خاله ↔ شوهرخاله

دختر دائی — پسر دائی — دختر خاله — پسر خاله

خویشاوندان پدری

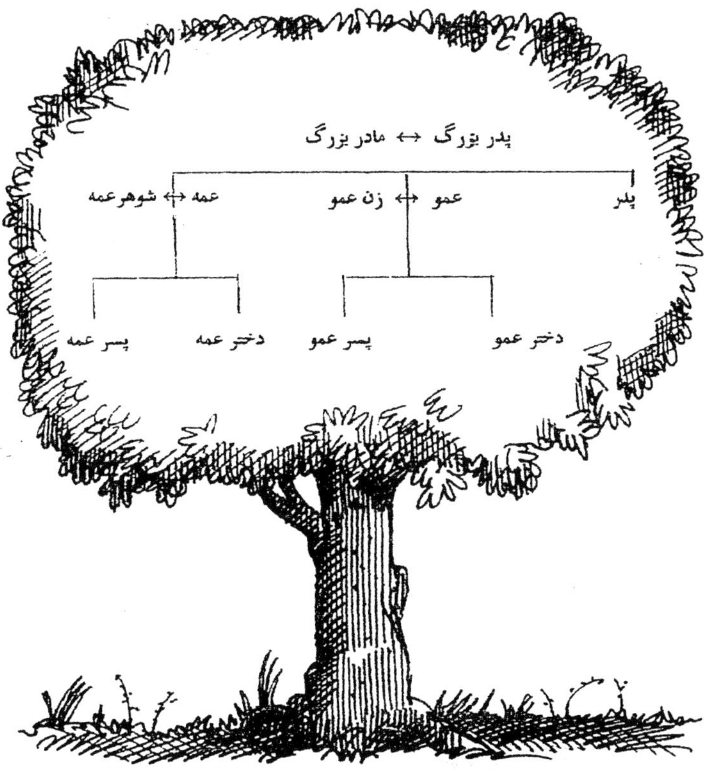

گفتگو

مینا	ببخشید آقا، شما دانشجو هستید؟
نادر	بله، من دانشجو هستم.
مینا	چه می خوانید؟
نادر	تاریخ و فارسی می خوانم.
مینا	دوستتان چه می خواند؟
نادر	کدام دوستم؟
مینا	دوست ایرانی تان آقای فرشاد.
نادر	ایشان زبان شناسی می خواند.
مینا	خانمشان چه می خواند؟
نادر	کتابداری می خواند.
مینا	کتابداری سخت است یا آسان ؟
نادر	کتابداری سخت نیست، خیلی جالب است.

elementary/ high school student.	دانش آموز
college / university student	دانشجو
college	دانشکده
university	دانشگاه
teachers college	دانشسرا
diploma, university degree	دانشنامه

خواندن

خانواده آذری

آقای اردشیر آذری و همسر ایشان، خانم مینا آذری، دو فرزند دارند، یک پسر به نام مهرداد و یک دختر به نام شهرزاد. مهرداد ده سال دارد و دانش آموز کلاس چهارم دبستان فردوسی است. شهرزاد سه سال از برادرش مهرداد کوچکتر است. شهرزاد دانش آموز کلاس دوم دبستان پروین اعتصامی است.

خانواده آذری در تهران زندگی می کنند. آقای آذری دبیر زبان انگلیسی دبیرستان فردوسی است. خانم آذری کتابدار است و هفته ای سه روز در کتابخانه دانشگاه تهران کار می کند.

خواندن

دیروز یک نامه از برادرم رابرت داشتم. رابرت شش سال از من بزرگتر است. تابستان سال پیش به ایران رفت و در تهران کار گرفت.

رابرت در ایران دوستان زیادی دارد. یکی از دوستانش آقای بیژن ثریاست. من بیژن را خوب می شناسم، سال پیش که در آمریکا بود با هم در یک خانه زندگی می کردیم.

بیژن تابستان گذشته از دانشگاه میشیگان دکترا گرفت و به ایران برگشت. او حالا در دانشگاه تهران کار می کند، استاد زبان انگلیسی است.

پرسش:

۱ـ رابرت کی به ایران رفت؟

۲ـ در کجا کار گرفت؟

۳ـ بیشتر دوستان رابرت کجائی هستند؟

٤ـ یکی از دوستان ایرانی او را نام ببرید.

٥ـ اسم کوچک آقای ثریا چیست؟

٦ـ بیژن از کدام دانشگاه دکترا گرفت؟

۷ـ دانشگاه میشیگان در کدام شهر آمریکاست؟

۸ـ آیا حالا بیژن در ایران درس می دهد؟

۹ـ در کدام دانشگاه درس می دهد؟

از

مثلهای فارسی

۱ـ پارسال دوست امسال آشنا.

۲ـ باد آورده را باد می برد.

1. Long time no see.
   (It is said ironically to a rather cold friend who has not been seen for a long time.)
2. Easy come easy go.

از

اصطلاحات فارسی

۴ـ زود باش!

۵ـ وقت تنگ است.

3. Hurry up!
4. There is no time to lose.

Dictation

As you are listening to the CD, fill in the missing words.

ما هفته ای ....ساعت کلاس فارسی داریم.

کلاس فارسی ما هر روز ساعت ده ....

می شود و ده و پنجاه................................ تمام می شود.

در کلاس ما دوازده................................ هست، هفت

دختر و پنج پسر. کلاس فارسی ما در طبقه دوم ساختمان ادبیات است.

ساختمان ادبیات رو به روی ....مرکزی دانشگاه است.

Write the following words under each picture.

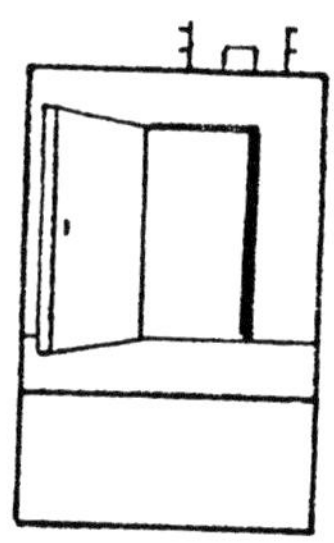

۱

۲

۳

٤

٥

٦

Listening Comprehension

Listen to the pre-recorded conversations. The conversations are followed by a few statements. Determine whether the statements are true or false. Write درست for true and غلط for false.

۱. --- ۲. --- ۳. --- ۴. ---

۱. --- ۲. --- ۳. ---

You will hear a Persian anecdote. Then you will be asked to listen to a few statements to determine whether they are true or false according to the story.

سخنرانی

یک شب مردی سخنرانی می کرد. سخنرانی او آن قدر طولانی و خسته کننده شد که عده ای از شنوندگان رفتند. آنها هم که ماندند خوابشان برده بود. وقتی که آن مرد سخنرانیش تمام شد، به صدای بلند پرسید: «خوب، سؤالی ندارید؟»

در این وقت، یکی از شنوندگان، که تازه از خواب بیدار شده بود چشم هایش را مالید و گفت: «چرا آقا، ساعت چند است؟»

۱. --- ۲. --- ۳. --- ۴. ---

یادداشت های انگلیسی

Family

The family bond is very strong in Iran and provides its member with their identity, security, and social organization. The father is the head of the family and the mother is the center of the home. Home life revolves around her. In general, parents have a great deal of authority over their children, especially when they are very young. Many children are taught at an early age to respect their parents and older members of the family.

In Iran, the family consists of not only father, mother, and their children; but also grandparents, uncles, aunts, cousins, nephews, nieces' and in-laws. There are close ties to members of the family, and the younger members of the family eventually take care of older relatives. Many members of the family live in the same household. Even if they live in different homes they prefer to be in the same neighborhood and always maintain close ties with each other. Members of the family are usually consulted when it comes to making major decisions.

Young adults usually live in their parents' home when they are in school. However, they may leave the parent's home for college education in another town. Parents also support their children's .educational expenses. Young Iranians often consult their parents in pursuing a particular profession, getting married, and other life-shaping decisions. Although nowadays young adults choose their own spouses, they still seek the approval of their parents

All in all, the family bond is still the strongest source of stability and identity in Persian society. Children who grow up in a large family feel secure in an extended family.

First Names Adopted as Family Names

Certain first names commonly used for boys and girls may be adopted for family names. The use of titles of address خانم – آقا with first names designates the family names. A short list of such names illustrates the point.

آقای آذر	خانم آذر
آقای اشرف	خانم اشرف
آقای بیژن	خانم بیژن

Additional examples of this type of names include the following:

پرتو	همایون
سروش	بهنام
کیوان	مهران

Suffixes that are frequently used in Persian family names include the following:

- ی /i/ "related to, pertaining to"

  احمدی تبریزی

- پور "son, daughter"

  ایران پور امان پور

- زاد or زاده "offspring"

  فرخ زاد رضا زاده

- نیا "ancestor, forefather"

  بزرگ نیا اکبر نیا

Prepositions

Prepositions are a short list of words which relate a noun (its object) to other words in the sentence. There are two types of prepositions as listed below

- A) Prepositions that are not followed by the connective اضافه

to	به
with	با
of, from	از
in	در
without	بی
until	تا
except	مگر
except	جز

- B) Prepositions that are followed by the connective اضافه

behind	پشتِ
between	بینِ
for	برایِ
below	پائینِ
above	بالایِ
near	نزدیکِ
between	میانِ
at	سرِ

Compound Prepositions

Words such as بیرون از 'out of'' and پیش از'before', are interpreted as one unit, a single preposition and they are called compound prepositions. A short list of compound prepositions includes the following:

in front of	رو به روی
after	بعد از
about	درباره
towards	به طرفِ
before	پیش از
before	قبل از
in between	درمیانِ
instead of	بجای

Prepositions with Verbs

Verbs in Persian regularly appear in combination with certain prepositions. Picking the right preposition is often due to an idiom .

حرف زدن	با
جواب دادن	به
پرسیدن	از
رسیدن	به
خوش آمدن	از
نگاه کردن	به

The Simple Past Tense

This tense is formed from the past stem plus the verb endings, but in the third person singular only the stem is used.

	Plural	Singular
1st	رفتیم	رفتم
2nd	رفتید	رفتی
3rd	رفتند	رفت

Uses of the Simple Past

Most frequently the simple past tense is used to designate a completed action taking place at a definite point in the past as in,

من دیشب با دوستم به سینما رفتم.

I went to the movies with my friend last night.

Other uses of the simple past include the following:

When using the adverbial denoting a period of time, the simple past tense can express either continuous or a repeated action as illustrated in the examples below.

- In subordinate clauses when the tense of the main clause is present/future as in:

وقتی درس تمام شد به آزمایشگاه زبان می رویم.

When the lesson is over we will go to the language laboratory.

اگر به دوستتان نامه نوشتید سلام مرا به ایشان برسانید.

If you write a letter to your friend say hello to him for me.

وقتی به انگلیس رفتید از موزه بریتانیا دیدن کنید.

When you go to England visit the British Museum.

- In certain idiomatic constructions, the simple past tense may point to a future action, or an action that is about to happen as illustrated in the following examples:

سلام خانم، با آقای راد کار داشتم.

Hello Miss, I need to talk to Mr. Rad.

Durative Past

Durative past is formed from the past stem plus the prefix می . The verb form is used for continuous action in the past as illustrated in the following:

من و پرویز چند سالی در ایران کار می کردیم.

Parviz and I used to work in Iran for a few years.

This form of the past tense is also used to express unreal actions as in,

اگر زودتربه آزمایشگاه زبان رفته بودید،

استاد فارسی را در آنجا می دیدید.

If you would have gone to the language laboratory earlier, you would have seen the Persian professor.

Or

اگر زودتر به‌آزمایشگاه زبان‌می رفتید

استاد فارسی را در آنجا می دیدید.

If you would have gone to the language laboratory earlier, you would have seen the Persian professor.

Simple vs. Compound Verbs

There are two types of verbs in Persian, simple and compound. A verb is simple when it is formed from a single word (the verb stem plus the prefixes and the verb ending) as in,

می خوانید	بخوانید	نخوانید
می روید	بروید	نروید
می نویسیم	بنویسید	ننویسید

Compound verbs consist of two parts. The first part, which is invariable, is called the preverb as in the following examples:

گوش دادن

حرف زدن

از دست دادن

برپاکردن

The second part, the verbal, is inflected for tense, number, person and other grammatical categories, e.g.,

امروز صبح به دوستم تلفن کردم.

I called up my friend this morning.

من با او خیلی حرف زدم.

I talked to him a lot.

The first part of the compound verbs may be a simple word as in دست دادن 'to shake hands', حرف زدن 'to talk' or more than one word as in از دست دادن 'to lose', بر پاکردن , 'to establish', رو به رو شدن 'to face', etc.

The following observations should be made about compound verbs in Persian:

- The number of compound verbs is large, and they considerably outnumber simple verbs.
- The total meaning of the preverb and the verb is often different from that of the constituent as in,

برپا کردن.

- Compound verbs are usually translated into one-word verb English, e.g.,

زمین خوردن

- In compound verbs, the stress falls on the final syllable of the preverb when the verb is affirmative. In the negative form, the stress falls on the prefix نَ of the verb.
- Various parts of speech may be employed as a preverb, as in the words listed below.

a) nouns

b) adjectives

c) prepositions

d) adverbs

- Words of Arabic, Turkish, and Western origin often function as preverbs.

a) Arabic شروع کردن

b) Turkish قاچ کردن

c) English تلفن کردن

عربی در فارسی

Arabic in Persian

Arabic elements used in Persian are of various types.

Simple Words

Some of the simple Arabic words that frequently appear in Persian include the following:

سلام	حال	اسم
ساعت	ربع	خبر
سؤال	جواب	درس
کلمه	جمله	عدد

Compound Words

In the formation of compound words Arabic words are used with Persian words, as illustrated below:

فارسی + عربی

خوشحال (خوش + حال)

هیچوقت (هیچ + وقت)

پرمعنی (پر + معنی)

عربی + فارسی

کتابخانه (کتاب + خانه)

خبرنامه (خبر + نامه)

اسم نویسی (اسم + نویسی)

Derived Words

Persian prefixes and suffixes are often used with Arabic words, e.g.,

پیشوند فارسی + کلمه عربی
با + خبر
نا + شُکر
نَ + فهم

کلمه عربی + پسوند فارسی
مصر + ی
خطر + ناک
عین + ک

Exclamatory Sentences

This type of sentence is used to express emotions or feelings. e.g.,

چه اتاق گرمی! این اتاق برای زمستان خوب است.

What a warm room! This room is good for the winter.

In the structure of exclamatory sentences note the following features:

- The exclamatory sentences are often introduced by چه "what a", which forms a statement.
- In writing, exclamatory sentences end with an exclamation mark.
- In spoken Persian, they are recognized by tone of voice.
- The verb may be omitted in these type of sentences, e.g.,

چه اتاق گرمی!

چه اتاق گرمی است!

تمرین و تکلیف

A. Matching

Match the definitions read to you with the words listed below the definitions. Write the corresponding number in the blank spaces.

۱. سی یا سی و یک روز است.

۲. در ایران روز اوّل هفته است.

۳. روز تعطیل هفته است.

۴. هفت روز است.

۵. گرمترین فصل سال

۶. سه ماه از سال

۷. در دانشگاه به ما درس می دهد.

۸. جای آزمایش و تمرین زبان

۹. در دانشگاه درس می خواند.

۱۰. برادر مادر

۱۱. مرد زن دار

۱۲. خواهر پدر

۱۳. خواهر مادر

۱۴. چهار فصل دارد.

۱۵. اتاق درس

۱۶. پایتخت ایران

۱۷. سردترین فصل سال

۱۸. برادر پدر

--- هفته

--- ماه

--- تابستان

--- فصل

--- دانشجو

--- آزمایشگاه زبان

--- عمو

--- عمه

--- سال

--- شنبه

--- شوهر

--- تهران

--- زمستان

--- خاله

--- دائی

--- کلاس

--- استاد

--- جمعه

B. Categorization

Look at the graphic of the family tree and check the kinship terms under appropriate columns.

Relatives through marriage	Father's side	Mother's side	Kinship terms	
			عمو	۱
			خاله	۲
			پدر بزرگ	۳
			دائی	۴
			داماد	۵
			دختر خاله	۶
			زن عمو	۷
			مادر بزرگ	۸
			عروس	۹
			زن دائی	۱۰
			پسر عمو	۱۱
			شوهر عمه	۱۲

C. Review of Compound Verbs

The following simple infinitives in English are translated into compound infinitives in Persian. In the blank spaces provided, write the two Persian constituents of the compound verbs as in the example given.

Example: to speak	زدن	حرف
1. to live	________	________
2. to open	________	________
3. to end	________	________
4. to begin	________	________
5. to teach	________	________
6. to return	________	________
7. to fix	________	________
8. to practice	________	________
9. to wait	________	________
10. to learn	________	________
11. to listen	________	________
12. to like	________	________
13. to find	________	________
14. to look at	________	________
15. to decide	________	________
16. to remove	________	________

D. Translation

First translate the following questions into Persian. Then give responses in spoken st of Persian.

1. How many brothers and sisters does your Iranian friend have?

____

2. Where do your friend's parents live?

____

3. Is your Iranian friend older or younger than you?

____

4. What is your Iranian friend's first name?

____

5. In which building is the history class?

____

6. Which one of your classes are in the library?

____

7. Is the university library a three-story building?

____

8. How about the university bookstore?

____

G. Group Sentence Building

The first student says a word that would come at the beginning of a Persian sentence. The next student adds a word that would logically follow in a proper Persian sentence. Other students continue to add words until a meaningful grammatical sentence is created.
Example.

Student A says:	من
Student B says:	یک
Student C says:	دوست
Student D says:	ایرانی
Student E says:	دارم.
Student F says:	اسم
Student G says:	او
Student H says:	پرویز
Student I says:	نادری
Student j says:	است.

من یک دوست ایرانی دارم.

اسم او پرویز نادری است.

Situation Card # 5

For the first time, you are going to meet Robert's family at their home. Be prepared to ask:

1. How many brothers and sisters he has.
2. Whether his brothers and sisters are married.
3. If he has uncles and aunts.
4. Whether he lives close to his relatives
5. How often he gets to see his close relatives.

Finally, tell Robert that one day you will introduce him to his family.

Situation Card # 6

You have come to the Persian instructor's office to inquire about the intermediate Persian course.

1. Greet her.
2. Introduce yourself and tell her about your language background.
3. Ask when the intermediate Persian class meets; in the morning or in the afternoon.
4. Find out on which days and in which building the class meets.
5. Tell her that you have already signed up for the intermediate Persian course.
6. Ask her about the instructional materials that are adopted for the course. Take note of the list of instructional materials.
7. Say goodbye.

Situation Card #7

Parviz received a letter from his sister. Politely ask him the following:

1. From where he received the letter.
2. Who wrote him the letter.
3. Where his sister lives.
4. What her job is.
5. Whether she is younger or older than he.
6. How well she knows English.

Pair Practice

a) Fill in your weekly class schedule on the calendar. Show your calendar to a classmate and ask him/her to ask you about your weekly schedule.

b) Outline and briefly explain your daily schedule to a classmate. Then ask him/her questions concerning his/her daily schedule.

c) Assume that you have arrived late to the class. Explain to your instructor a major excuse beyond your control for your tardiness.

جدول

از راست به چپ

۱ـ قسمتهای سخت درخت

۲ـ رطوبت، تری

۳ـ آواز خواندن و نواختن ساز

٤ـ روشنائی

۵ـ سه بعلاوه پنج

٦ـ بسته نیست.

از بالا به پائین

۷ـ رودخانه ای است که از اهواز می گذرد.

۸ـ زمین سبز

۹ـ رنگ طلائی، زرد یا سرخ کمرنگ

۱۰ـ یکی از فلزات قیمتی است.

۱۱ـ شراب

۱۲ـ آخرین ماه سال ایرانی

۱۳ـ میوه ای است خوشمزه ،

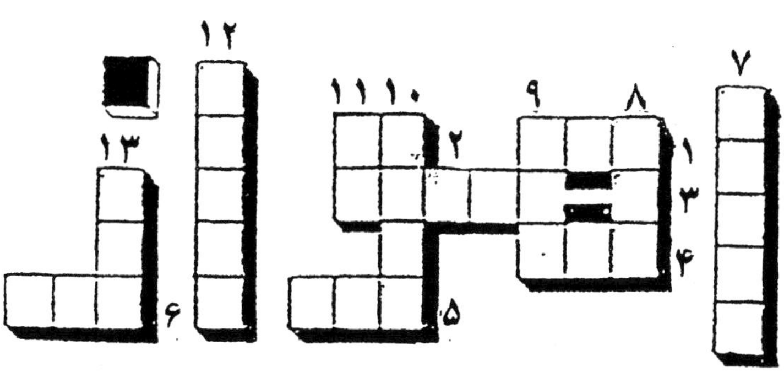

استان خوزستان

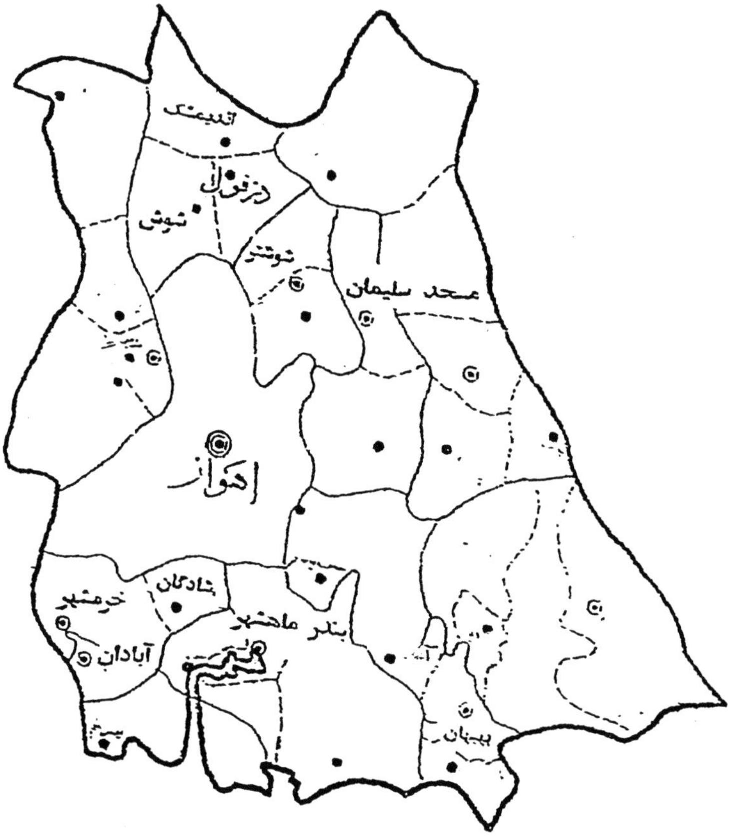

این شهرها را روی نقشه خوزستان پیدا کنید.

اهواز	خرمشهر	آبادان	شوش
شوشتر	اندیمشک	بهبهان	آغاجاری
دزفول	شادگان	مسجد سلیمان	

درس پنجم

۱- خواندن - گفتگو

سفری به واشنگتن

مسافرت به ایران

۲- گفتگو - خواندن

در باره هوا

از داستانهای ملاّ نصرالدین

املا - چند دستور املائی

۳- دستور زبان

باید - خواستن - توانستن

حروف اضافه - زمان گذشته -

ماضی نقلی - ماضی بعید - زمان آینده

۴- تمرین و تکلیف

معنی انگلیسی	کلمه‌های تازه
travelling	مسافرت...........
empty...............	خالی................
to stop............	توقف کردن.......
ship................	کشتی................
train...............	قطار.................
airplane	هواپیما.............
car................	ماشین (اتومبیل)
memorial....	یاد بود..............
test	امتحان...............
to decide ..	تصمیم گرفتن.....
to leave	حرکت کردن.......
of course ..	البته..................
to drive	رانندگی کردن......
tired	خسته ....
stay	اقامت................
to last	طول کشیدن........
museum ...	موزه....................
mosque	مسجد...................

خواندن

سفری به واشنگتن

هفته گذشته امتحانات ما تمام شد و دانشگاه چند روزی تعطیل بود. از این رو من و دوست ایرانیم، بیژن، تصمیم گرفتیم به واشنگتن مسافرت کنیم.

صبح روز شنبه با اتومبیل به طرف واشنگتن حرکت کردیم و بعد از بیست و چهار ساعت به آن شهر رسیدیم. البته شب در یکی از مهمانخانه های بین راه خوابیدیم ولی تقریباً در تمام روز رانندگی می کردیم.وقتی بیژن خسته می شد من رانندگی می کردم.

اقامت ما در شهر واشنگتن یک هفته طول کشید. در این مدّت از موزه ها، کتابخانه ها و بسیاری جاهای دیگر دیدن کردیم. یک روز هم به مسجد این شهر رفتیم. این مسجد بسیار جالب توّجه است.

مسجد

پرسش:

به سوالهای زیر جواب بدهید.

۱ـ بیژن و دوستش به کدام شهر مسافرت کردند؟

۲ـ آیا با اتومبیل مسافرت کردند یا با هواپیما؟

۳ـ چند ساعت در راه بودند؟

٤ـ اقامت آنها در واشنگتن چقدر طول کشید؟

۵ـ در واشنگتن از کجا دیدن کردند؟

٦ـ آیا از مسجد واشنگتن هم دیدن کردند؟

۷ـ شما تا کنون به واشنگتن مسافرت کرده اید؟

۸ـ کتابخانه کنگره آمریکا در شهر واشنگتن است؟

۹ـ سازمان ملل در کدام شهر آمریکاست؟

۱۰ـ یونسکو در کدام شهر اروپائی است؟

مسافرت به ایران

فرهاد: جین، تابستان کجا بودی؟

جین: رفته بودم پیش دوستم مینا.

فرهاد: پدر و مادر مینا کجا زندگی می کنند؟

جین: در تهران زندگی می کنند.

فرهاد: خوب، چند وقت تهران ماندی؟

جین: تقریباً یک ماه.

فرهاد: خوش گذشت؟

جین: بله.خیلی خوش گذشت.جای شما خالی بود.

فرهاد: دوستان به جای ما. هوا چطور بود؟ مثل اینجا گرم بود؟

جین: بله، گرم بود.

فرهاد: کی از ایران برگشتید؟

جین: هفته پیش با هواپیما برگشتیم.

فرهاد	اروپا توقف نکردید؟
جین	چرا، دو روز لندن و چهار روز پاریس بودم.

True/false Statements.

۱ .... جین تابستان به ایران مسافرت کرده بود.

۲ .... اسم دوست ایرانی جین میناست.

۳ .... پدر و مادر مینا در اصفهان زندگی می کنند.

٤ .... جین تمام تابستان را در ایران ماند.

۵ .... جین با هواپیما به آمریکا برگشت.

٦ .... جین در اروپا سه هفته از دوستانش دیدن کرد.

۷ .... جین در ایتالیا و اسپانیا هم توقف کرد.

۸ .... هوای تهران در تابستان گرم نبود.

۹ .... جین در اروپا توقف کرد.

کلمه های هم معنی

ماندن	توقف کردن
برگشتن	مراجعت کردن
پرسیدن	سؤال کردن
دراز	طولانی
زمان	وقت

درباره هوا

پرویز	سلام مریم.
مریم	سلام پرویز، حالت خوب است؟
پرویز	بد نیست. متشکرم.
مریم	راستی دیشب برف آمد؟
پرویز	بله، خیلی برف آمد.
مریم	فردا هوا چطور است؟ فردا هم برف می آید؟
پرویز	نخیر، رادیو گفت آفتابی است.
مریم	اینجا زمستان خیلی برف می آید؟
پرویز	نه، گاهی برف می آید ولی بیشتر باران می آید.
مریم	تابستان هوا چطور است؟
پرویز	کمی گرم است ولی مرطوب نیست.

چهار فصل سال

بهار تابستان پاییز زمستان

پرسش:

۱ـ اینجا زمستان برف می آید؟

۲ـ تابستان هوا چطور است؟

۳ـ هوای بهار ملایم است یا گرم است؟

٤ـ هوای تابستان خشک است یا مرطوب است؟

۵ـ پائیز خیلی باران می آید؟

٦ـ امروز هوا چطور است؟

۷ـ دیشب باران آمد؟

۸ـ فردا آفتابی است یا ابری است؟

***

۹ـ حد اکثر درجه گرما در این شهر چیست؟

۱۰ـ حداقل درجه سرما در تهران چیست؟

۱۱ـ در کدام فصل بیشتر باران می آید؟

۱۲ـ در کدام فصل روزها بلند می شود؟

۱۳ـ در کدام فصل روزها کوتاه می شود؟

١٤ـ در کدام فصل روز و شب برابر می شود؟

۱۵ـ معمولاً در چه فصلی برگ درختان می ریزد؟

خواندن

فردا هوا چگونه خواهد بود؟

بارها از خود یا دیگران می پرسیم که « فردا هوا چگونه خواهد بود؟» آیا فردا می توانیم برای پیاده روی به پارک شهر برویم؟ آیا روز جمعه آفتابی خواهد بود و مسابقه فوتبال برگزار خواهد شد؟ راستی سیزده فروردین امسال هوا چگونه خواهد بود؟

آیا می توانیم بدون چتر و بارانی سیزده به در را در خارج از شهر بگذرانیم؟ آیا برف چند روز پیش به اسکی بازان اجازه می دهد به آبعلی بروند؟

ابری

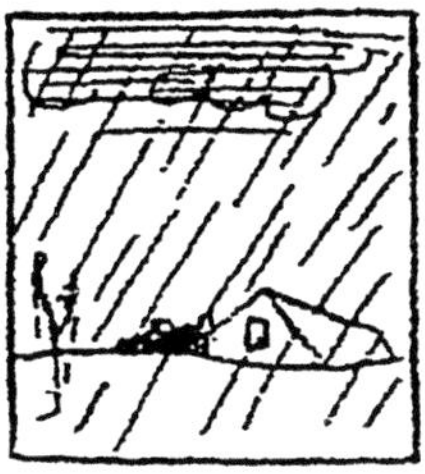

بارانی

آفتابی

تقریباً همه ما در برنامه روزانه خود به وضع هوا توّجه می کنیم. در بعضی از کارها، پیش بینی وضع هوا بسیار لازم است. مثلاً رانندگان اتومبیل شخصی، رانندگان اتوبوس و تاکسی، هوانوردان و کشاورزان به پیش بینی هوا بسیار توّجه می کنند.

بخوانید و بخندید!

از داستانهای

ملّا نصرالدین

پولم همینجا گم شده بود.....

چقدر تاریکه!

آها... فهمیدم چه جوری پیدایش کنم.

زن ملّا: ملّا دنبال چه می گردی؟

ملّا: دنبال پولم.

زن مّلا: کجا گمش گردی؟

مّلا: توی حیاط ... ولی چون اونجا

تاریک بود اومدم تو روشنی پیدایش کنم.

املا

Dictation

As you are listening to the tape, fill in the missing words.

پیش بینی هوای تهران در   ساعت آینده

اداره هواشناسی دانشگاه تهران...............................

می دهد که هوای تهران و شهرهای.......................... آن

در روز سیزدهم.............................. پیش از ظهر کمی مه

آلود است و در ———— لکه های ابر دیده می شود.

بر طبق پیش بینی هواشناسان .... آفتابی

است. روز چهاردهم تمام روز هوا......................... و

آفتابی است. حداقل درجه حرارت در روزهای سیزدهم

وچهاردهم ....درجه و ....

سی و یک درجه سانتیگراد خواهد بود.

Additional words.

۱ ____________ ۲ ____________

۳ ____________ ٤ ____________

۵ ____________ ٦ ____________

۷ ____________ ۸ ____________

۹ ____________ ۱۰ ____________

چند دستور املائی

۱ـ کلمه های این و آن را جدا بنویسید. مانند:

این پسر را نمی شناسم.

آن دختر را خوب می شناسم.

یادآوری: در چند کلمه این دستور بکار نمی رود. مانند:

اینجا

آنجا

آنچه

۲ـ نشانه را جدا نوشته می شود، مانند:

ایشان را در مهمانی دیشب ندیدم.

یکی را انتخاب کنید.

کتاب را از کتابفروشی خریدم.

یادآوری: در چند کلمه این دستور بکار نمی رود. مانند:

چرا (چه + را) مرا (من + را)

۳ـ نشانه های جمع را پیوسته بنویسید، مانند:

گلها درختان

سالها زنان

یادآوری: اگر حرف آخر کلمه (ه) ، نشانهٔ کسرهٔ اضافه باشد، نشانهٔ جمع را جدا بنویسید. مانند:

خانه ها نامه ها دانشکده ها همسایه ها

دستور زبان

Modals in Persian

Wish, desire, resolutions, command and condition are expressed in Persian by adding modals to the main verbs as illustrtated in the following sentences.

من امشب می خواهم با دوستم به سینما بروم.

ما حالا می توانیم فارسی بخوانیم و بنویسیم.

لطفاً این جمله های انگلیسی را به فارسی بنویسید.

Note:

- Modals precede the main verbs in the sentence.
- The present stem of the main verb takes the prefix ب .
- In contemporary Persian باید 'must' is invariable with all persons, e.g.,

باید بروم	باید بروی	باید برود
باید برویم	باید بروید	باید بروند

- خواستن and توانستن match the main verb in person and number and they take the prefix می e.g.,

می خواهم بخوانم	می خواهی بخوانی	می خواهد بخواند
می خواهیم بخوانیم	می خواهید بخوانید	می خواهند بخوانند

- The negative prefix normally occurs with the modal as in following examples:

پدرم از این پس نمی تواند کار کند.
My father cannot work hereafter.

در این ساختمان نباید سیگار بکشید.
No smoking in this building.

قهوه نمی خواهم، چای لطف کنید.
I don't want coffee. Please give me tea.

The Meanings of Modals

In general modals are used to express actions and events that exist in the mind of the speaker. The meanings of the modal auxiliaries are best understood in the context of discourse. The following sentences should help you understand the meanings od modals in Persian.

توانستن

- is used primarily to express ability, e.g.,

برادرم می تواند به سه زبان انگلیسی، آلمانی و ترکی ترجمه کند.

(He is able to….)

Other meanings of the verb include the following:

- Permission

می توانم پنجره را ببندم؟

(Do you permit me to…..?)

- Possibility

استاد ما بعد از ظهر کلاس ندارد. ایشان می تواند شما را ببیند.

(It is possible that….)

خواستن

- Future Activity

تابستان آینده به ایران خواهم رفت.

- Promise

بدون شک به ایشان کمک خواهم کرد.

- Desire

دلم می خواهد هرچه زودتر شما را ببینم.

باید is used as an invariable form with all persons.

- Necessity

سخنرانی باید سر وقت شروع شود.

The lecture must begin on time.

- Obligation

ما باید وقت شناس باشیم.

We ought to be punctual.

- Deduction

شما امروز خیلی کار کرده اید، باید خسته باشید.

You have worked hard today. You must be tired.

Note:

- Modals precede the main verbs in the sentence.
- The modals خواستن and توانستن like main verbs are inflected for person, number, tense, negation and the prefix /mi/.
- In contemporary Persian باید is used invariably with all persons/numbers combinations and the tense distinction between باید and بایست is no longer made,
- Modals are not used with another member of their own class, whereas sequence of verbs proper are possible.

The Present Perfect Tense

In Persian, the present perfect tense consists of the past participle of the main verb with the short form of "to be" - ام، ایم، ای، اید، اند with the exception of the third person singular in which است is used. The pattern of the conjugation of the present perfect tense is as follows:

Affirmative

رفته ام	رفته ایم
رفته ای	رفته اید
رفته است	رفته اند

Negative

نرفته ام	نرفته ایم
نرفته ای	نرفته اید
نرفته است	نرفته اند

Note that:

- The present perfect tense is used to refer to an act, which is still in progress. In other words, it links past with the present, e.g.

من یک سال فارسی خوانده ام.

I have studied Persian for a year.

استاد فارسی ما سالها در آمریکا زندگی کرده است.

Our Persian professor has lived in the U.S. for years.

- In rapid pronunciation, the suffix (-e) of the past participle and the glottal stop drop out and the vowel of the auxiliary verb 'to be' is heard longer than usual.

- In spoken Persian, the present perfect tense is distinct from the simple past tense with regard to the position of stress.

- The past participle, which is used in the formation of the present and past perfect is formed by adding the suffix (-e) to the past stem of the verbs, e.g.,

Past Participle	Past Stem
رفته	رفت

The Past Perfect Tense

The past perfect is compounded of the past participle of the main verb plus the past tense of "to be". For example:

رفته بودیم	رفته بودم
رفته بودید	رفته بودی
رفته بودند	رفته بود

- The past perfect normally refers to a time farther in the past than another past time, e.g.,

وقتی که به ایستگاه رسیدم قطار حرکت کرده بود.

When I arrived at the station the train had left.

- The past perfect may be replaced by the simple past when the two events occur in a relatively quick sequence, e.g.

وقتی که به ایستگاه رسیدم قطار حرکت کرد.

When I arrived at the station the train left.

- The negative form of the past perfect is formed by adding the negative prefix to the past participle of the main verb, e.g.,

نرفته بودم

ننوشته بودم

زمان آینده

The Definite Future

You have already noted that the simple present tense has both present and future meaning as illustrated in the following examples:

امروز از ساعت ده تا ظهر کار می کنم.
I work from ten to noon today.
فردا از ساعت ده تا ظهر کار می کنم.
I'll work from ten to noon tomorrow.

The definite future is formed by adding the present stem of **خواستن** "to want" to the short infinitive of the main verb.

خواه + پسوند فعل + مصدر کوتاه

Note that:

- The auxiliary **خواستن** does not take the prefix **می** in this usage.
- The verb endings are used with the auxiliary verb **خواستن** "to want" to mark persons and numbers.
- The negative of the definite future is formed by adding the negative prefix **ن** to the auxiliary verb. The negative forms of the definite future are as follows:

نخواهم رفت	نخواهیم رفت
نخواهی رفت	نخواهید رفت
نخواهد رفت	نخواهند رفت

Compare the paradigm of the simple present tense with the definite future.

Definite Future	Simple Present
خواهم آمد	می آیم
خواهی آمد	می آیی
خواهد آمد	می آید
خواهیم آمد	می آئیم
خواهید آمد	می آئید
خواهیم آمد	می آئیم

Additional examples:

Definite Future	Simple Present
خواهم رفت	می روم
خواهی خواند	می خوانی
خواهد نوشت	می نویسد
خواهیم خورد	می خورم
خواهی بست	می بندی

In compound verbs the future auxiliary خواستن precedes the short infinitive of the main verb as in the following

برادرم بزودی از آمریکا به ایران باز خواهد گشت.

My brother will soon return from the U.S. to Iran.

تمرین و تکلیف

A. Reading Signs

Study the following traffic signs and say what they tell you to do when you see them on the street.

گردش به چپ ممنوع

سیگار نکشید

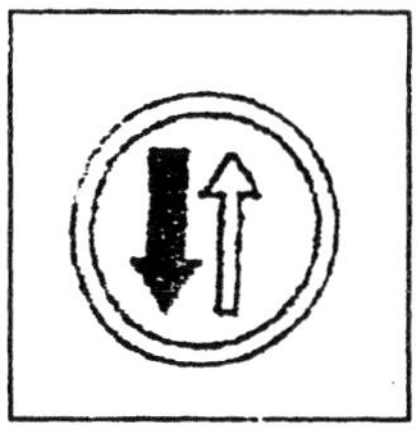

جاده دو طرفه

دور نزنید

آهسته برانید

بوق نزنید

B. Fill in the blanks

جاهای خالی را با فعل توانستن پرکنید:

نمونه: شما می توانید به من کمک کنید؟

۱) ما حالا ------- فارسی بخوانیم و بنویسیم.

۲) دوست ایرانیم مترجم خوبی است. او ----- به چند زبان حرف بزند و ترجمه کند.

۳) ببخشید خانم، شما----- این نامهٔ فارسی را به انگلیسی ترجمه کنید؟

٤) ----- امضا و نشانی فرستنده نامه را بخوانید؟

جاهای خالی را با فعل (خواستن) پرکنید:

٦) فریدون -------- سال آینده به اروپا و ایران مسافرت کند.

۷) من و دوست ایرانیم، بیژن، ------- تابستان آینده به کنار دریا برویم.

۸) برنامه امسال تابستان شما چیست؟ آیا -------- کار کنید یا به دانشگاه بروید؟

۹) من ----- هفته ای فقط سه روز کار کنم.

۱۰) تو و رابرت -------- چه کار کنید؟

C. Reading the Weather Chart

Study the following graph before you write your answers to the questions in Persian.

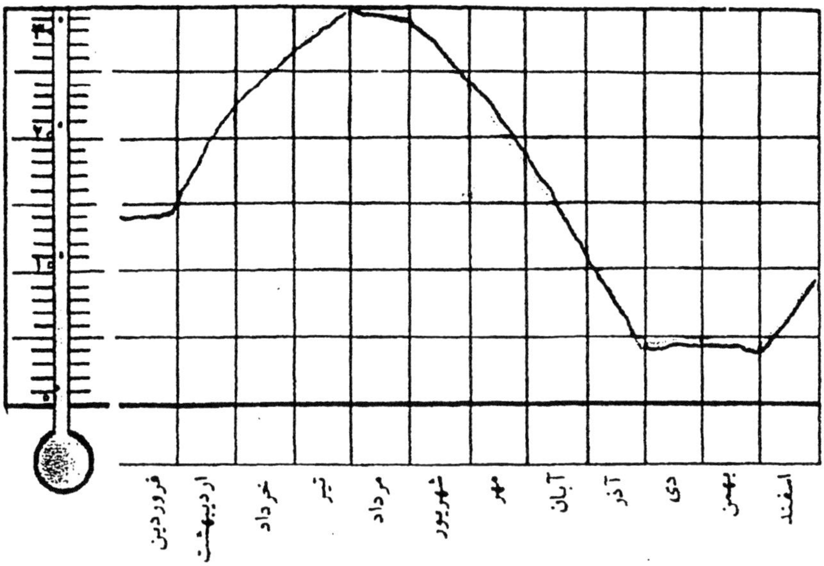

۱ـ منحنی بالا چه چیزی را نشان می دهد؟

....

۲ـ دمای تهران در چه ماههائی به حداقل می رسد؟

....

۳ـ گرمترین روزهای تهران در چه ماههائی از سال است؟

....

٤ـ دمای تهران در ماه فروردین چگونه است؟

....

۵ـ در چه ماههائی هوای تهران ملایم است؟

....

D. Centigrade vs. Fahrenheit

a) Study the following conversation to figure out how to convert Centigrade to Fahrenheit.

استاد می دانی امروز درجه حرارت چیست؟

دانشجو رادیو گفت ۸۰ درجه فارنهایت است.

استاد بگو ببینم به سانتیگراد چقدر می شود؟

دانشجو ببخشید نمی دانم.

استاد خوب گوش کن! اول ۳۲ را از ۸۰ کم کن ، می شود ۴۸، بعد این عدد را در پنج ضرب کن می شود ۲۴۰، عدد ۲۴۰ را به ۹ تقسیم کن تقریباً می شود ۲۷ درجه سانتیگراد.

دانشجو از راهنمایی شما متشکرم.

b) Do the following conversion.

Centigrade	**Fahrenheit**
0^0	______
5^0	______
10^0	______
15^0	______

E. Reading Comprehension

Read the following anecdote silently. Then determine which of the four topics listed below best describes the story.

جوانی پس از آنکه مدّت هفت سال پیش یک استاد زبان انگلیسی خوانده بود برای خداحافظی پیش او رفت و گفت: استاد از زحمتی که در این مدّت برایم کشیده اید سپاسگزارم. خواهش می کنم اگر خدمتی از دست من بر می آید بفرمائید تا با کمال میل برایتان انجام بدهم.

استاد گفت: خیلی ممنونم. از شما فقط یک خواهش دارم و آن این است که به کسی نگوئید که پیش من انگلیسی یاد گرفته اید.

Suggested topics:

الف ـ خواهش بی جا

ب ـ جوان درس خوان

ج ـ پرسش بجا

د ـ خواهش استاد

تمرین و تکلیف

F. Translation

Orally translate the following questions in colloquial style. Then write your responses in written standard Persian.

1. Has your Iranian friend, Nader, taken a trip to Iran?

____

2. How did he go to Iran?

____

3. How long did he stay in Iran?

____

4. Have you recently heard from him?

____

5. When is he coming back?

____

6. Has he already bought his return ticket?

____

7. Have you ever taken a trip to Europe?

____

Situation Card #8

You and your friend are at Homa Travel Agency in London (Speak for both of you).

1. Tell the travel agent that you wish to go to Tehran. You need two round trip tickets.
2. Explain that you wish to leave London this coming week and return a month later.
3. Ask how many flights to Tehran there are next week.
4. Inquire if the flights to Tehran are nonstop.
5. Ask the price for the cheapest tickets available.
6. Ask if you can pay with your credit card.

Situation Card #9

You have just returned from a trip, and you want to tell Mina all about it.

1. Greet Mina and tell her that you were on vacation in Europe. Tell her that you were also in Canada for a month.
2. Tell Mina that you love Ottawa. Explain to her that it is a wonderful city.
3. Tell her that you stayed in a friend's house.
4. Explain to Mina that you were able to practice your French while in Canada.
5. Ask Mina if she has been to Canada.
6. Show Mina a map of Canada. Point out the places you visited.

جدول

خانه های جدول را پر کنید .

۱ - مرکزاستان مازندران .

۲ - پایتخت ایتالیا .

۳ - شهری است بین تهران و اصفهان .

۴ - زبان رسمی افغانستان .

۵ - قطار مسافری یا باری .

۶ - ریشه زمان حال فعل «رسیدن» .

۷ - مردم این شهر به لهجه یزدی حرف می زنند .

۸ - مرکزاستان گیلان .

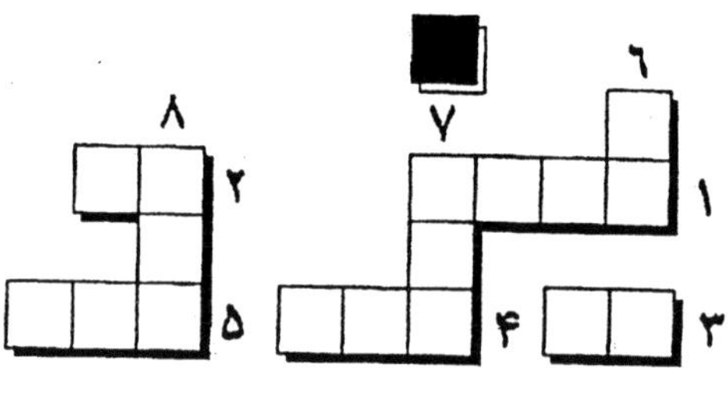

درس ششم

۱ـ گفتگو

ناشتائی، ناهار، شام

چرا فارسی می خوانید؟

۲- خواندن

برنامه روزانه آقای ایرانی

از داستانهای ملّا نصرالدین

۳ـ یادداشتهای انگلیسی

٤ـ دستور زبان

چند دستور املائی

۵ـ تمرین و تکلیف

کلمه‌های تازه	معنی انگلیسی
غذا........................	food..........................
خوش.................	good, pleasant..........
فعلاً.....................	right now.................
گرسنه..................	hungry.....................
آب میوه...............	fruit juice................
خوشوقت............	glad.........................
تا..........................	until.........................
معمولاً..................	usually....................
کتابخانه................	library.....................
صبحانه.................	breakfast................
شام.........................	dinner.....................
عصر.......................	late afternoon ....
زبان شناسی...........	linguistics..............
کتابداری................	library science........
سخت.....................	difficult..................
آسان......................	easy.........................

ناشتائی ناهار شام

لیلی	آقای وفائی. کجا دارید می روید؟
فرهاد	دارم میروم رستوران دانشگاه ناهار بخورم.
لیلی	شما از غذای رستوران دانشگاه خوشتان می آید؟
فرهاد	بله، غذایش بد نیست. شما ناهار خورده اید؟
لیلی	نخیر، نخورده ام ولی فعلاً گرسنه ام نیست.
فرهاد	پس رستوران نمی آئید؟
لیلی	چرا، می آیم . می خواهم یک لیوان آب میوه بخورم.
فرهاد	خوب، بفرمائید با هم باشیم. خیلی خوشوقت می شوم.

لیلی   متشکرم آقای وفائی.

فرهاد   راستی، بعد از ظهر کلاس دارید؟

لیلی   نخیر، ولی معمولاً می روم کتابخانه.

فرهاد   تا کی کتابخانه می مانید؟

لیلی   تا ساعت چهار، بعد می روم منزل.

چرا فارسی می خوانید؟

مریم	ببخشید آقا، شما دانشجو هستید؟
سیروس	بله، من دانشجوی این دانشگاه هستم.
مریم	در این دانشگاه چه می خوانید؟
سیروس	فارسی و تاریخ می خوانم.
مریم	چرا فارسی می خوانید؟
سیروس	چون فارسی زبان خارجی من است. بعلاوه می خواهم به ایران بروم و درباره تاریخ مشروطّیت ایران مطالعه کنم.
مریم	چرا تاریخ مشروطّیت؟

سیروس چون این موضوع را برای رساله
دکترا انتخاب کرده ام.

مریم شما تاکنون به ایران رفته اید؟

سیروس بله، دو مرتبه به ایران رفته ام و یک
سال و نیم در دانشگاه تهران فارسی
خوانده ام.

مریم برنامه دکترای شما چقدر طول
می کشد؟

سیروس درست نمی دانم. اگر امسال در
امتحان دکترا قبول شوم به ایران
می روم و رساله دکترا را در آنجا
می نویسم.

مریم به نظر شما این کار چقدر طول
می کشد؟

سیروس به نظرم یک سال کافی است.

مریم بعد به آمریکا بر می گردید؟

سیروس بله، در نظر دارم بعد از گرفتن
دکترا دریکی از دانشگاهها درس
بدهم. من از کار در دانشگاه
خوشم می آید.

از

مثلهای فارسی

۱ـ سیر از گرسنه خبر ندارد.

۲ـ خواستن توانستن است.

۳ـ شنیدن کی بود مانند دیدن.

1. The full man does not understand a hungry one.
2. Where there is a will, there is a way.
3. Seeing is believing.

از

اصطلاحات فارسی

٤ـ راستی؟

٥ـ حالش جا آمد.

4. Really?
5. He came to his senses.

معنی انگلیسی	کلمه‌های تازه
program..........	برنامه ....
employee........	کارمند......................
center.............	مرکز.........................
to ride.............	سوار شدن..............
to wash...........	شستن......................
to study...........	مطالعه کردن............
present............	حاضر...................
customer..........	مشتری..................
colleague..........	همکار...................
kind.................	مهربان..................
to behave..........	رفتار کردن.............
to take a rest.....	استراحت کردن.......
to need.............	لازم داشتن.............
to dream...........	خواب دیدن...........
dark.................	تار...........................

خواندن

برنامه روزانه آقای ایرانی

آقای ایرانی کارمند بانک مرکزی ایران است. او هر روز ساعت هفت از خواب بیدار می شود. دست و روی خود را می شوید، لباس می پوشد و آنگاه صبحانه می خورد. پس از آن روزنامه های صبح را مطالعه می کند.
آقای ایرانی خیلی وقت شناس است. همیشه ساعت نه سرکار خود حاضر می شود و با مشتریان بانک و همکاران خود به مهربانی رفتار می کند. آقای ایرانی ساعت دوازده به رستوران بانک می رود و با دوستان همکار خود ناهار می خورد.
ساعات اداری بانک از نه صبح تا چهار بعد ازظهر است. بنابراین آقای ایرانی ساعت چهار به خانه بر می گردد، قدری استراحت می کند و با خانم ایرانی درباره کار روزانه گفتگو می کند، بعد شام می خورند. خانم و آقای ایرانی غالباً شبها در منزل استراحت می کنند، گاهی به دیدن دوستان خود می روند، ولی هر شب ساعت یازده و نیم می خوابند.

یادداشت های انگلیسی

Food

Persian dishes are usually prepared with herbs and spices, making them varied and quite delicious. Wheat bread, and rice are the staple foods of Iran. Bread is made with hard wheat and is well cooked. It comes in long strips or round pancakes, baked in different sizes and thicknesses. Iranians prefer eating bread straight out of the oven and even go to the market daily to purchase fresh, hot bread.

Rice is the essential element of Iranian cuisine. Great care is taken in preparing the rice, as it is rinsed several times and steamed before it is served. چلو کباب chelo-kabab is a favorite Iranian meal. It consists of grilled fillets of lamb served with plain rice or چلو 'chelo' and mixed with butter, egg yolk, powdered سماق (somāq), and slices of raw onion. دوغ 'duq' (yogurt diluted with carbonated water) is a refreshing cold drink that commonly accompanies chelo-kabab. Other meals are prepared with steamed rice and a variety of sauces made with meat, vegetables, seasoned plums, celery and currents, to mention a few.

Traditionally, the dining experience takes place on the floor. In modern day Iran, spoons and forks are used. The spoon is held in the right hand and the fork in the left. Meals at home are usually served from a table.

Along the Caspian Sea and Persian Gulf, fish is the main source of protein. These areas are famous for their seafood, especially sturgeon, from which the world's finest caviar is obtained.

Tea is the most common beverage. Iranians are very particular about the taste and the aroma of the tea. Water is boiled in سماور /samāvar/ and tea is allowed to draw in قوری, which is placed on the top of سماور.

. سماور

چای

املا

به نوار کاست گوش کنید و کلمه های از قلم افتاده را بنویسید.

برادر عزیزم بیژن!

امیدوارم سلامت و خوب و ----- باشی. حالا درست چهار ماه است که به آمریکا ------ . دوری از تو و ------- و برادرانم برایم سخت است. ------- رسید. نمی دانی چقدر از ------- آن خوشحال شدم. از من خواسته ای که از برنامه زندگی ام در آمریکا برایت بنویسم. هفته آینده که دانشگاه چند روزی ------ است نامه مفصلی برایت می نویسم در اینجا با تو ------- می کنم. از قول من به همه فامیل و دوستان سلام برسان.

Now translate the following words into Persian.

1	post office	
2	stamp	
3	envelope	
4	mail box	
5	address	

i. Answer the questions you hear on the tape.

ii. Listening Comprehension

a. 1.--- 2. ---- 3. ---- 4. ----

b. 1.--- 2. ---- 3. ---- 4. ----

c 1.--- 2. ---- 3. ---- 4. ---- 5. ----- 6. -----

iii. Vocabulary

Listen to the tape and check under a, b, c or d that correspond to the English translation listed in your book.

#		a	b	c	d
1	engineer				
2	oil company				
3	typist				
4	uncle				
5	mother tongue				
6	return				
7	Friday				
8	to lose				
9	drill				
10	anthropology				

از داستانهای

ملاّ نصر الدین

ملاّ : زن ، بیدار شو، بیدار شو، با تو هستم .

زن ملاّ: چکار داری، مرا بیدار کردی؟

ملاّ: عینکم را بده لازمش دارم.

زن ملاّ: این وقت شب.عینکت را چکار داری؟

ملاّ : آهان ، داشتم خواب خوبی می دیدم کمی تار بود. گفتم عینکم را بزنم تا بهتر ببینم.

دستور زبان

The Functions of خود

- Emphasis

In this usage خود matches the English 'myself, yourself, himself, etc', and it is used for emphasis as in:

من خود داستان را به تو گفتم.

I myself told you the story.

In contemporary Persian, خود is used in combination with suffixed pronouns, e.g.

من خودم	ما خودمان
تو خودت	شما خودتان
او خودش	ایشان خودشان

In written Persian, however, خود is invariable in form for all persons. Note that when خود stands with a pronoun, a noun or a modifier, it takes the connective /e/ Ezafe as in the following sentence.

خودِ آقای ایرانی این خبر را به من داد.

Mr. Irani himself gave me the news.

- **Reflexive خود**

خود may be used as a reflexive pronoun when the action of the verb is pointed back to the subject of the sentence as in the following example. (Notice that the subject and the object are the same person.)

من خود را به حاضران معرفی کردم.

I introduced myself to the audience.

- Modifier

In addition to the above functions, خود may also be used as a modifier, e.g.,

آقای ایرانی ناهار را با دوستان خود می خورد.

Mr. Irani takes lunch with his friends.

The Present Progressive Tense.

The verb داشتن 'to have', which as a main verb indicates possession, can be employed as an auxiliary in the formation of progressive tenses. Compare the two functions of داشتن in the following sentences.

الف – من یک برادر دارم.

I have one brother.

ب – من حالا دارم نامه می نویسم.

I am writing a letter now.

In sentence الف the verb دارم 'I have' is the main verb; in sentence ب the main verb is می نویسم 'I write' and دارم expresses the grammatical category of progressive events. The conjugation of the present progressive tense is as follows:

دارم می روم	داری می روی	دارد می رود
داریم می رویم	دارید می روید	دارند می روند

The Past Progressive Tense

The past progressive is composed of the past tense of the auxiliary داشتن and the past stem of the main verb. The verb endings of the auxiliary match the endings of the main verbs in:

داشتم می رفتم	داشتی می رفتی	داشت می رفت
داشتیم می رفتیم	داشتید می رفتید	داشتیم می رفتیم

The past progressive corresponds closely in use to the present progressive. The present progressive indicates an event as progressing through the present moment; the past progressive indicates an event as progressing through a specific period in the past.

چند دستور املائی

۱ـ حرف « و» در بعضی کلمه ها بعد از « خ » نوشته می شود ولی تلفظ نمی شود مانند:

خواهر

خواهش

خواب

خواندن

۲ـ حرف « ی » در آخر بعضی کلمه ها « آ » تلفظ می شود مانند:

حتّیٰ

موسیٰ

عیسیٰ

یحییٰ

مجتبیٰ

۳ـ حرف اضافه « به » را جدا بنویسید مانند:

به نام خدا

کی به تو فارسی یاد می دهد؟

۴ـ پیشوند « می » را جدا از فعل بنویسید مانند:

می نویسیم

می بینید

۵ـ پیشوند « هم » را بر سر اسم پیوسته بنویسید. مانند:

همکار

همشهری

همسر

همکلاسی

٦ـ پیشوند « بی » را که بر سر اسم می آید جدا بنویسید. مانند:

بی ادب

بی انصاف

بی پول

یادآوری: در چند کلمه پیشوند « بی » را باید پیوسته نوشت. مانند:

بیچاره

بیهوده

۷ـ پیشوند « ب » را که بر سر فعل می آید به ان بچسبانید مانند:

بنویسید

بخوانید

ببندید

بیائید

۸ـ پیشوند « ب » را که بر سر اسم در می آید پیوسته بنویسید مانند:

بنام

بجا

نابجا

۹ـ واژه های مرکب را پیوسته بنویسید مانند:

کتابخانه

حسابدار

کتابدار

خوشبخت

یادآوری : فعلهای مرکب را جدا بنویسید مانند:

نگاه کردن

زمین خوردن

تمرین و تکلیف

A. Questions and Answers

Use the appropriate forms of the present progressive tense in your response to the following questions.

۱ـ این پسر دارد چکار می کند؟

۲ـ بچه ها دارند بازی می کنند؟

۳ـ پرویز دارد لباس می پوشد؟

٤ـ این آقا دارد در کتابخانه چکار می کند؟

۵ـ این پسر دارد جورابش را از روی زمین بر می دارد؟

٦ـ دانش آموزان دارند به دبستان می روند یا به دبیرستان؟

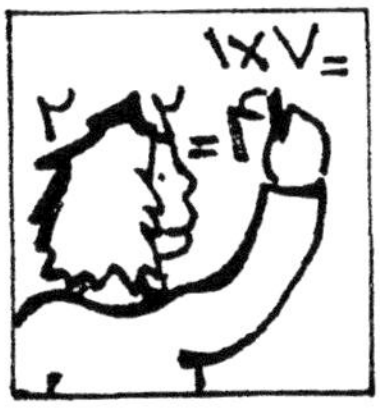

۷ـ این پسر دارد روزنامه می خواند یاحساب می نویسد؟

۸ـ این دانشجویان دارند در آزمایشگاه زبان به نوار فارسی گوش می دهند؟

B. Content Areas

Cross out the word in each line that does not belong.

Content Area	ه	د	ج	ب	الف	#
هوا	باد	مرطوب	زبان *	برف	باران	۱
	میوه	کباب	خشک	چلو	تخم مرغ	۲
	لطفاً	رادیو	متشکّرم	بفرمائید	ببخشید	۳
	قطار	تاکسی	کتابخانه	کشتی	هواپیما	۴
	پدر	دانشجو	مادربزرگ	خاله	دائی	۵
	سال	ناشتائی	فصل	هفته	ماه	۶
	گرسنه	کوکاکولا	قهوه	چای	آب میوه	۷
	عصر	ظهر	شب	روز	غذا	۸
	خودنویس	گچ	قلم	مداد	رستوران	۹
	زمستان	پائیز	تابستان	صندلی	بهار	۱۰
	مرطوب	سرما	گرم	تلویزیون	آفتابی	۱۱
	دوچرخه	اتوبوس	ساعت	قایق	ماشین	۱۲
	داماد	عمه	خداحافظ	عمو	برادر	۱۳
	مصری	ترک	افغانی	آمریکا	تاجیک	۱۴
	پشتو	فارسی	دری	اردو	دبیرستان	۱۵

C. Questions and Answers

الف ـ آقای مارتین هر روز ساعت چند از خواب بیدار می شود؟

ب ـ شما معمولاً ساعت چند از خواب بیدار می شوید؟

ج ـ دوستتان کی از خواب بیدار می شود؟

الف ـ آقای‌مارتین هر روز ساعت چند صبحانه می خورد؟

ب ـ شما معمولاً ساعت چند صبحانه می خورید؟

ج ـ شما در منزل صبحانه می خوردید یا در رستوران؟

الف ـ آقای مارتین کی روزنامه های صبح را مطالعه می کند؟

ب ـ شما معمولاً روزنامه های صبح را مطالعه می کنید؟

الف ـ آقای مارتین هر روز ساعت چند به اداره می رود؟

ب ـ شما معمولاً ساعت چند به سر کار خود می روید؟

الف ـ خانم و آقای مارتین ساعت چند شام می خورند؟

ب ـ شما معمولاً ساعت چند شام می خورید؟

ج ـ کجا شام می خورید؟ در منزل یا در رستوران ؟

الف ـ خانم و آقای مارتین هر روز ساعت چند به رادیو گوش می دهند؟

ب ـ شما معمولاً ساعت چند به اخبار رادیو گوش می دهید؟

الف ـ آقای مارتین هر روز ساعت چند می خوابد؟

ب ـ شما معمولاً ساعت چند می خوابید؟

معنی مخالف کلمه های زیر را بنویسید.

۱ـ خوابیدن ____________

۲ـ کار کردن ____________

۳ـ هرگز ____________

۴ـ روز ____________

۵ـ گرسنه ____________

D-Twenty Questions بیست سؤالی

One student is selected to leave the class. The remaining students and the instructor choose an object in the classroom. The student comes back into the room and begins to ask a series of 'yes' or 'no' questions in Persian in order to find out what the object is.. The student can ask up to 20 questions, and the one who guesses correctly is the winner.

An Example of Questions and Answers:.

۱. در شمال ایران است؟ نخیر

۲. در مشرق است؟ نخیر

۳. رودخانه است؟ نخیر

٤. کوهستان است؟ نخیر

۵. یکی از دهات ایران است؟ نخیر

٦. از شهرهای کوچک ایران است؟ نخیر

۷. در مغرب ایران است؟ نخیر

۸ . از شهرهای پرجمعیت ایران است؟ بله

۹. رودخانه ای از نزدیک آن می گذرد؟ نخیر

۱۰. در چهار فصل سال، آب و هوای ملایمی دارد؟ بله

۱۱. خلیج فارس در جنوب آن قرار دارد؟ بله

۱۲. یکی از شهرهای قدیمی ایران است؟ بله

۱۳. مر کز استان است؟ بله

۱۴· مرکز استان خوزستان ؟ نخیر

۱۵· اسم آن با حروف ش شروع می شود؟ بله

۱۶· شهر شیراز است؟

آفرین درست است،شهر شیراز است·

Situation Card # 10

You and your Iranian friend are at a Persian restaurant.

1. Tell the waiter that you would like to take a table for two, and near the window.
2. Tell the waiter that both you and your friend will have chelo kabab cucumber-yogurt, and salad with olive oil, vinegar and pepper.
3. For drink, order a pitcher of duq.
4. Ask the waiter to bring you some more bread and onion.
5. Pay the bill to the cashier, and thank the waiter.

Situation Card # 11

You are buying a teapot and some tea in the grocery store.

1. Tell the shopkeeper that you want to buy a medium-size teapot.
2. Ask him for a white and blue teapot that is not too expensive.
3. Find out how much the teapot costs.
4. Ask the shopkeeper that you also need half a kilo of sugar and 250 grams of tea.
5. The shopkeeper gives you tea from China; explain to him that you prefer tea from India.
6. Find out how much the tea and the sugar will cost.
7. Ask him to calculate the total cost. Pay the bill, and thank him for his help.

Situation Card # 12

Mina is visiting your Persian class.

1. Ask her politely to come to the front of the class.
2. Introduce her to the class. Mention her name, her hometown in Iran, her field of study and languages she speaks.
3. Ask her to locate her hometown on the map of Iran.
4. Ask her to say a few words about her hometown.
5. Inquire about the climate, the population, the neighboring towns, and the main occupation of her townsmen.
6. Thank her for visiting your class.

جدول

از راست به چپ

۱ـ ماه دهم از سال ایرانی

۲ـ روزی که بیشتر مردم ایران به بیرون شهر می روند.

۳ـ یکی از کلمه های پرسشی است که برای زمان به کار می رود.

٤ـ مذهب

۵ـ آن را به نشانه سلامتی روی سفره هفت سین می گذارند.

از بالا به پایین

٦ـ بسیار

۷ـ رساله

۸ـ آخ، افسوس

۹ـ بین دو کوه قرار دارد.

۱۰ـ پرآب است.

۱۱ـ مهمترین جشن ایرانیان

۱۲ـ آن را می خوانیم.

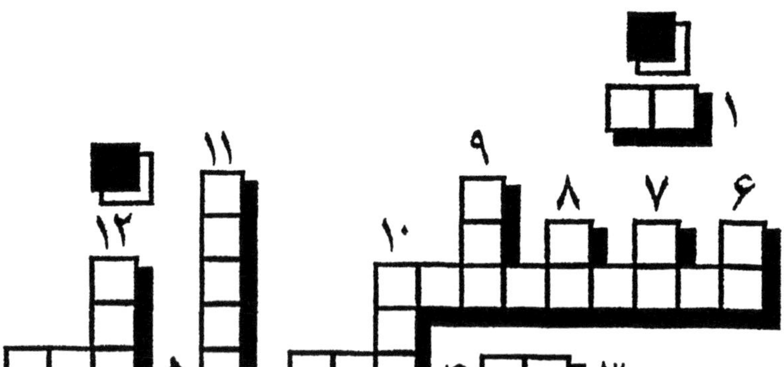

درس هفتم

۱ـ گفتگو

تولّدت مبارک!

۲ـ خواندن

شعر تولّد

از مثل های فارسی

۳ـ دستور زبان

مصدر عربی در فارسی

صفات برتر و برترین

انواع قید

٤ـ تمرین و تکلیف

معنی انگلیسی	کلمه‌های تازه
invitation	دعوت
relatives	بستگان
on the occasion of	بمناسبت
to arrange	ترتیب دادن
surprise	غافلگیر
suggestion	پیشنهاد
coincident	مصادف
congratulations	تبریک
gift	هدیه
agreeing	موافق
intensive	فشرده
carrying on	برگزار کردن
advanced	پیشرفته
at present	فعلاً
discount	تخفیف

تولّدت مبارک

پرویز بچّه ها راستی می دانید که هفته آینده روز تولّد مریم است؟

روشنک آره، اتفاقاً برادر مریم دیشب به من تلفن کرد و گفت قرار است جمعه شب بچّه های فامیل منزل خاله پروین جمع بشوند و تولد مریم را جشن بگیرند.

پرویز دوستان مریم هم دعوت دارند؟

روشنک فکر نمی کنم چون این یک مهمانی خانوادگی است فقط بستگان نزدیک مریم برای شام دعوت دارند.

پرویز خوب، پس چطور است ما هم به مناسبت روز تولّد مریم ترتیبی بدهیم و مریم را غافلگیر کنیم. شماها چه فکر می کنید؟

آذر من پیشنهاد می کنم روز جمعه آینده که مصادف با روز تولّد مریم و آخرین روز سال تحصیلی است برای ناهار دور هم جمع شویم و تولّد مریم را به او تبریک بگوئیم.

پرویز با این پیشنهاد موافقید؟

امیر به نظر من پیشنهاد خوبی است. می توانیم در یکی از اتاق های باشگاه دانشجویان به بهانه خداحافظی آخر سال تحصیلی دور هم جمع بشویم و بلافاصله بعد از ناهار با خواندن ترانه تولد مریم را حسابی غافلگیر کنیم.

آذر من با این پیشنهاد موافقم و حاضرم ترتیب گرفتن اتاق را بدهم. می دانید من هفته ای دو روز در رستوران دانشگاه کار می کنم وبا کارمندان باشگاه آشنائی دارم.

روشنک من هم حاضرم کیک تولّد را درست کنم.

نادر ترتیب نوشابه، بستنی، شمع، بشقاب، کارد و چنگال و دستمال سفره هم با من.

پرویز خوب بگوئید ببینم برای هدیه تولّد چکار کنیم؟

آذر به نظر می آید بجای اینکه ما تک تک به مریم هدیه بدهیم بهتر است از طرف کلاس یک هدیه خوبی برایش تهیه کنیم.

پرویز امیر تو چه پیشنهادی می کنی؟

امیر من با نطر آذر موافقم و حاضرم در جمع آوری پول و خرید آلبوم کمک کنم.

پرویز روشنک تو چه فکر می کنی؟

روشنک تا آنجائی که من خبر دارم مریم در نظر دارد امسال تابستان در برنامه فشرده زبان عربی شرکت کند و خودش را برای امتحان عربی دوره لیسانس آماده کند. چطور است برایش آلبوم جدید نوارهای عربی دانشگاه آمریکائی بیروت را بخریم.

پرویز بچّه ها با این پیشنهاد موافقید؟

نادر بـه نـظرم پیشنهاد جالـبی است. چون مریم می تواند با استفاده از این نوارها خودش را برای امتحان عربی که آخر تابستان برگزار می شود آماده بکند.

پرویز خوب، نادر ممکن است اطلاعاتی درباره البوم نوارهای عربی به ما بدهید.

نادر بسیار خوب، این البوم شامل هشت ساعت مکالمه و خواندن عربی در سطح پیشرفته است. قیمت اصلی این آلبوم صد و بیست دلار است، ولی فعلاً در کتابفروشی آن را با تخفیف چهل درصد می فروشند.

پرویز چه خوب. پس از امیر خواهش می کنیم ترتیب خرید نوارهای عربی را بدهد.

امیر با کمال میل. در ضمن کاست ترانه تولد را هم می آورم تا دسته جمعی آن را برای مریم بخوانیم و تولّدش را به او تبریک بگوئیم.

Listening Comprehension

Listen to the passage before you determine whether the statement are true or false.

1. ---- **2.** ---- **3.** ---- **4.** ---- **5.** -----

ترانه تولّدت مبارک

تولّد،تولّد، تولّدت مبارک
مبارک، مبارک، تولّدت مبارک
بیا بندازیم* امشب یه عکس یادگاری
همه شب چه قشنگ شد چو غنچه بهاری
اشک شادی شمعُ نگاه کن
که واسات* بچکه* چکه چکه
کام همه را بیا شیرین کن
بیا کیکُ ببر تکه تکه
همه دور تو جمع گشته اند ای جان
گل بوسه می دهند تا بچینی
در جشن تولدت عزیزم
همه انگشترند تو نگینی
نگاه کن هدیه ها را
نگاه باد کنک ها را
همه رنگ و وارنگی
عجب شب قشنگی

---

* تلفظ گفتاری

زبان گفتار ـ زبان نوشتار

	colloquial form	written form	meaning
۱	بیا یه عکس بندازیم	بیا یک عکس بیاندازیم	let's take a picture.
۲	واسات	برای تو	for you
۳	بچکه	بچکد	drip
-	شمعُ	شمع را	the candle
۵	کیکُ ببر	کیک را ببر	cut the cake.

به تعریف این کلمه ها توجه کنید.

۱ـ یادگاری — چیزی که برای یاد بود به کسی بدهند.

۲ـ غنچه — گلی که هنوز باز نشده

۳ـ اشک — آب چشم

٤ـ شادی — خوشحالی، خوشی

۵ـ چکه — آب اندک که از جائی بچکد

٦ـ کام — دهان(سقف دهان)

۷ـ انگشتر — حلقه ای که در انگشت می کنند.

۸ـ نگین — سنگ قیمتی که بر روی انگشتر بنشانند.

۹ـ باد کنک — کیسه کوچک پلاستیکی که **آن را** باد می کنند تا در هوا پرواز کند.

۱۰ـ رنگ و وارنگ — به رنگ های گوناگون ، رنگارنگ

از
مثلهای فارسی

۱– نردبام پله پله

۲– عینک سواد نمی آورد.

1. Climb the ladder one step at a time.
   (He who would climb the ladder, must begin at the bottom.)

2. It is not the beard that makes the philosopher.
   (It is not the glasses that brings knowledge.)

از
اصطلاحات فارسی

۳– شتر دیدی ندیدی،

۴– توی دلم جا کرد.

3. Say you saw me not.

4. She won my heart.

دستور زبان

Inflection of Adjectives

Adjectives are inflected to show comparisons. The adjective بد 'bad' is called a positive form. The inflected form بدتر 'worse' and بدترین 'worst' are called comparative and superlative. The ending تر and ترین are added to the positive form for the comparative and superlative forms. The following are among the common adjectives in Persian.

big	بزرگ	۱
Small	کوچک	۲
dark	تاریک	۳
light	روشن	٤
warm	گرم	٥
cold	سرد	٦
old	پیر	۷
young	جوان	۸
short	کوتاه	۹
long	بلند	۱۰
easy	آسان	۱۱
difficult	سخت	۱۲
new	نو	۱۳
old	کهنه	۱٤

Note:

- Superlative adjectivers may appear in a few patterns as illustrated in the following sentences.

الف – تهران بزرگترین شهر ایران است.

ب – بزرگترین شهر ایران تهران است.

ج – تهران یکی از بزرگترین شهرهای ایران است.

د – تهران از همه شهرهای ایران بزرگتر است.

- In sentence (د) the comparative degree بزرگتر 'larger' is used with the expression همه 'all' to express the descriptive superlative.
- The suffixes تر and ترین receive stress.
- The preposition از in the above sentences matches 'than' in English.
- The comparative and superlative forms of some adjectives are irregular, e.g.,

good	خوب
better	خوبتر
best	خوبترین
much, a lot	بسیار
more	بیشتر
most	بیشترین

- Less common خوبتر and خوبترین are also used for بهتر and بهترین .

Types of Adverbs and Function:

Adverbs tell when, where or how an action occurred, e.g.,

الف – دیروز جشن تولّد مریم را در باشگاه دانشگاه برگزار کردیم.

ب – در این جشن که بخوبی برگزار شد بیشتر دوستان او شرکت داشتند.

In the above example, four types of adverbs appear in the statements. In the first statement the adverb of time دیروز tell us about the time of the birthday party, and the prepositional phrase در باشگاه دانشگاه about the place. Here, the adverbs of time and place modify the verb برگزار کردیم . In the second statement, بخوبی 'well' is an adverb of manner, which modifies the verb برگزار شد , and بیشتر is an adverb of quantity, modifying the verb شرکت داشتند. .

Adverbs in Persian tend to sort out into a few groups based on their meanings. These words answer the questions where?, when?, how much?, how?, etc. The following is a list of familiar adverbs.

Time	گاهی	الآن	بزودی	اکنون	حالا
	فوراً	هنوز	قبلاً	هرگز	همیشه
Place	بیرونِ	نزدیکِ	زیرِ	پائینِ	پیشِ
	نزدِ	میانِ	آنجا	راست	چپ
Quantity	بیش	بسی	اندک	کم	بسیار
Manner	سخت	خوب	بگرمی	تند	آهسته
Emphasis	فقط	حتّی	حتماً	ابداً	قطعاً

عربی در فارسی

Arabic Infinitives in Persian

Words such as تولّد 'bring forth, to give birth to'are Arabic infinitives used in Persian as verbal nouns. Arabic infinitives fall into certain patterns, and knowledge of these patterns and their meanings help to guess the meaning of Arabic words used in Persian.

The word تولّد is formed by the prefix ت and the three root consonants و ل د The general meaning of this pattern is action on oneself or for oneself . Additional examples of this pattern are listed in the grid. Study the formation and meaning of the words given.

to be born	زائیده شدن	تولّد	۱
being taught, learning	آموختن	تعلّم	۲
paying attention to	روگرداندن به طرف چیزی	توجّه	۳
to have mercy on somebody	مهربانی کردن	ترحّم	۴
embodiment	نمایان شدن	تجسّم	۵

Various types of Arabic infinitives, which appeared in the previous lessons include the following:

مکالمه مکاتبه ورود خروج شرح سلامت علم

تعلیم تربیت ادامه اتمام اعلام استفاده تدریس

Arabic infinitives are often followed by Persian verbals in compound verbs as illustrated in the following examples.

۱	توجّه کردن	to pay attention to	۳	حفظ کردن
۲	شرح دادن	to explain	۴	مکالمه کردن

تمرین و تکلیف

A. Finish the sentences

۱ـ وقتی وارد اتاق آقای رئیس شدم ایشان

....؟

(داشتند تلفن می کردند)

۲ـ وقتی زنگ مدرسه را زدند بچه ها

هنوز در مدرسه..............................؟

۳ـ بعد از آنکه از پرویز خداحافظی

کردم و به منزل رفتم او هنوز.......

....؟

٤ـ این دو دانشجو امروز صبح

در آزمایشگاه زبان.........................؟

۵ـ استاد فارسی ما پیش از کلاس

در اتاق کارش.......................؟

٦ـ وقتی امیر را صدا کردم.......

...................................؟

B. Categorization

Study the words listed below and categorize them in four groups by checking the appropriate column under A ,B ,C or D . The first one is done for you.

A. Polite expressions
B. Family
C. Nationalities
D. Weather

A	B	C	D	Words	#
			√	باران	۱
				بفرمائید	۲
				مرطوب	۳
				مصری	۴
				خاله	۵
				لطفاً	۶
				برف	۷
				متشکّرم	۸
				دائی	۹
				مکزیکی	۱۰
				ترک	۱۱
				تاجیک	۱۲
				آفتابی	۱۳
				ببخشید	۱۴

C. Guess the Word

The instructor asks the students to listen to each description and guess a word that matches each description. The game begins when the instructor makes a statement describing a words that begins with certain letter of the alphabet.

If someone succeeds in guessing, the instructor writes her/his name on the board ar gives the student a point. The game ends when twenty descriptions for twenty words have been used. The player with the highest point at he end is the winner.

بازی الفبا

(حرف م)

۱. در آب زندگی می کند. گوشت آن را می خوریم.

۲. سی یا سی و یک روز

۳. مادرِ مادر.

٤. واحد پول آلمان

۵. از شیر درست می شود. غذای مفیدی است که اسید لاکتیک دارد و برای سلامتی خوب است.

٦. ماه سوم از ماه فرنگی.

۷. پولی که دولت از مردم می گیرد.

۸. جانوری است که بدنش نرم است و روی زمین می خزد.

۹. کسی که زن و بچه دارد.

۱۰. واژه ای است فرانسوی. اسباب خانه مانند میز و صندلی و نیمکت با روپوش پارچه ای .

۱۱. کسی که سخنی را از زبانی به زبان دیگر ترجمه می کند.

۱۲. قطار زیر زمینی

۱۳. نام پیغمبر اسلام

۱٤. طرفی که آفتاب از آنجا بلند می شود.

۱۵. چشم انداز، دورنما

۱٦. ساختمانی که در آن آثار باستانی نگهداری یا به نمایش گذاشته می شود.

۱۷. مسلمانان در آنجا نماز می خوانند.

۱۸. کسی که پاره ای رشته های علمی را تحصیل کرده باشد.

۱۹. جانوری است از بسیاری صفات شبیه انسان. به آن آدم جنگلی هم می گویند. این جانوران غالباً در جنگلها روی درختان خانه می کنند.

۲۰. نام یکی از رشته های علوم انسانی است که درباره شناخت مردم و نژادهای مختلف و اخلاق و آثار آنها بحث می کند.

D. A Spelling Game

Directions: One student thinks of a Persian word, checks the correct spelling with the teacher, and goes to the chalk board. He draws a number of blanks on the board equal to the number of letters in the Persian word.

This student also draws a hangman's scaffold. The students take turns guessing the Persian letters for the word. With every incorrect guess, a part of the hanged person is drawn on the board, and the incorrect letter is written on the board. When the drawing is complete, the game is over.

Before all of the blanks are filled in, guessing the Persian word is allowed. An incorrect word guess also results in a part of the hanged man being drawn. The student who names the word wins, and thinks of a new word for the next game.

Example:

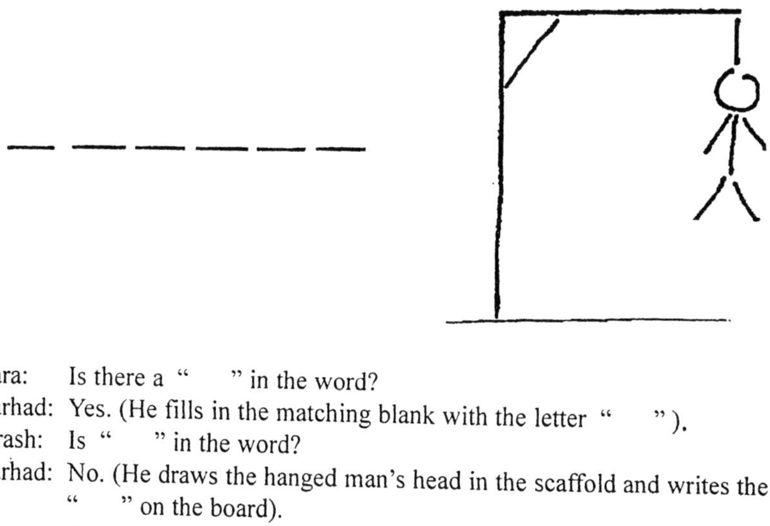

Sara: Is there a " " in the word?
Farhad: Yes. (He fills in the matching blank with the letter " ").
Arash: Is " " in the word?
Farhad: No. (He draws the hanged man's head in the scaffold and writes the letter " " on the board).
Azar: Is the word " "?
Farhad: Yes, you solved the puzzle. (He fills in the blanks with the correct Persian letters.

(Azar goes to the board and thinks of a new word and the game starts over).

E. Role Playing

Situation Card # 13

A classmate has invited you to go by car to a resort over the break. Ask about the following:

1. Time of departure.
2. Length of stay.
3. Cost of lodging, food, and gas.
4. Length of time it takes to get to the resort.
5. Points of interest near the resort.

Situation Card # 14

You are applying for a part-time job at the Middle East Library.

1. Greet the interviewer.
2. Explain that you saw an advertisement in the University's newspaper for a new library assistant for the Persian collection.
3. Explain why you are interested in the position.
4. Describe your qualifications.
5. Ask if you should provide references.
6. Ask about wages and the work schedule.
7. Thank the interviewer.

جدول

از راست به چپ

١ـ رنگ بالای پرچم ایران

٢ـ من + را

٣ـ 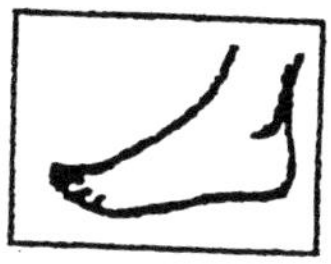

٤ـ به ما درس می دهد.

٥ـ چهار بعلاوه چهار (٤+٤)

٦ـ شب نیست.

٧ـ پایتخت ایران

از بالا به پایین

٨ـ نام گلی است خوشبو.

٩ـ 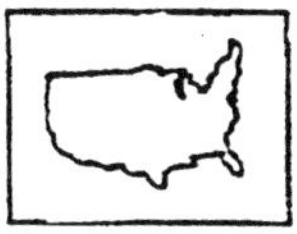

١٠ـ سی یا سی و یک روز است.

١١ـ زمان حال «بود»

١٢ـ والد

١٣ـ کشوری است در شمال آمریکا.

١٤ـ 

١٥ـ آن را می خوریم.

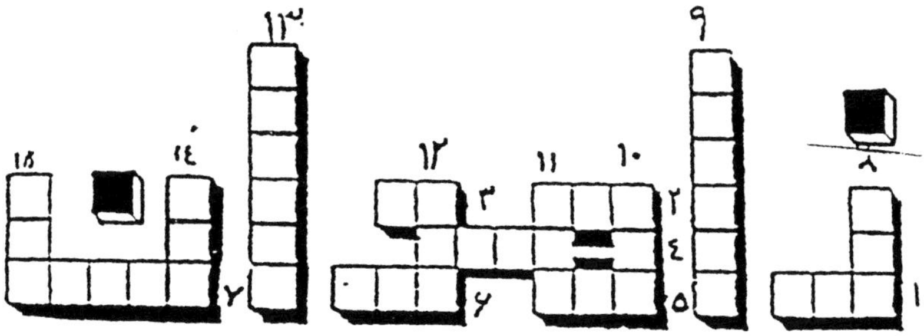

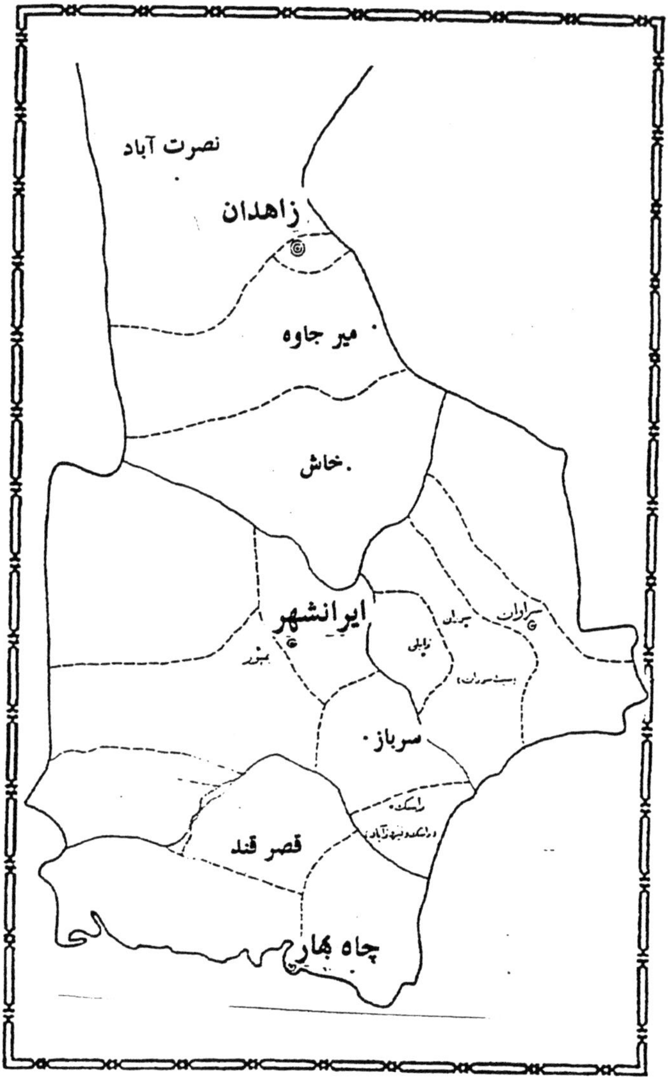

استان بلوچستان و سیستان

Proficiency in Persian

(*Book One*)

By:
Mehdi Marashi, Associate Professor Emeritus
The University of Utah,

In cooperation with
Latifeh Hagigi, Lecturer, Iranian Studies
University of California,
Los Angeles

Edited by:
Manouchehr Amiri
Dalia Yasharpour
Morteza Mortezai
Parvin and Ziba Marashi

Cover Design:
Ayyad Alnamar

The complete series of *Proficiency in Persian*, consisting of four textbooks and accompanying teaching aids, provides an integrated study program of materials for Persian studies.

Book One is intended to teach listening comprehension, speaking and reading at levels 0, 0+, 1 as defined by Interagency Language Roundtable (ILR) and American Council on Teaching Foreign Languages (ACTFL).

First edition 1991,
Library of Congress Registration # 385 037

Second edition 2007, ISBN # 0-9748018-0-1

For more information about the textbooks and the accompanying instructional materials contact:

sales@persianlanguageresources.com

Telephone 415-773-2123

For a complete list of products visit:
www.persianlanguageresources.com.

Contents

Contents of the Units

unit	a) Topic/Content	b) Function/Task
Introduction	- The Persian Alphabet - Names of the Letters - Variant Shapes of the Letters, Long vs. Short Form of the Letters - Dictionary Order of the Letters - Connectors vs. Non-Connectors - Similar Letters - Special Signs - The Arabic Letters - Letters and Sounds	- Recognizing the letters of alphabet - Pronouncing the names of the letters - Distinguishing the two sets of letters-connectors and non-connectors - Recognizing the function of the special signs - Matching letters with sounds - Copying simple words in familiar contexts - Reading legible handwriting
1	- Greetings and Leave-taking - In the Classroom - Where Is It? - At the Language Lab - Reading with Flashcards - Titles of Address - Colloquial vs. Written Persian - Role Play	- Rudimentary introduction - Exchanging social courtesies - Practicing colloquial Persian - Recognizing the letters of alphabet in words and short sentences - Reading sequence of short sentences - Talking about one's immediate environment – the classroom locating objects
2	- Self Introduction - Introducing Others - Languages, Nationalities and Countries - My Iranian Friend Ahmad - First Names in Persian - Numbers (11-20)	- Recognizing colloquial and standard written Persian - Using formal and informal greetings - Asking about peoples' nationalities, languages and countries

Contents of the Units

unit	c) Structure
Introduction	- The dictionary order of the letters - Combination of letters in words - Connectors and non-connectors - Letters with the same basic shape - The use of dots with the letters - Special signs - The Arabic letters - Sound value(s) of the letters - One letter – one sound - Multiple letters – one sound - One letter – multiple sounds - The spelling of vowels - The written and unwritten vowels
1	- The present tense of the verb 'to be' - Questions with question words how, who, what - Yes-no type questions - Basic prepositions - The present tense of the verb 'to have' - Verb endings - Pronunciation – vowels - Personal pronouns - Word order in statements
2	- The suffix /i/ - Pronunciation – syllable structure - Categories of first names in Persian - Persian consonants with no English counterpart - The verb stems of 'to be' - Patterns of Statements - Pronunciation – vowels - Personal pronouns

Contents of the Units

unit	a) Topic/Content	b) Function/Task
3	- Telling Time - Days of the Week - Formal and Informal Requests - Cardinal and Ordinal Numbers (1-100)	- Initiating conversation - Asking about time of the day, days of the week and dates of the month - Talking about daily routine - Reading class schedule - Understanding different types of quantities - Reading geographical maps - Asking for repetition - Making requests
4	- The Family - Family Relationships - Kinship Terms - Family Tree - Our Persian Class	- Discussing family relationships - Asking others about their family - Discussing immediate and extended family - Asking about relatives and friends - Reading a paragraph or two about past activities - Asking how to spell a word - Talking about our Persian class
5	- Traveling - Means of Transportation - Weather - A Persian Anecdote	- Planning a trip depending on the weather and season - Asking for transportation information - Discussing past summer vacation - Making hotel reservations - Expressing desire, wish and obligations - Expressing likes and dislikes

Contents of the Units

unit	c) Structure
3	- Cardinal and ordinal numbers (10-100) - Imperative sentences - Pronunciation of ه ل and ر - The plural suffixes - The connective /e/ اضافه - Request form of the verbs - Formal vs. informal requests - Verb endings - Present tense of the verb بودن 'to be', - Types of sentences
4	- Prepositions, simple and compound - Comparative degree of adjectives - Prepositions with verbs - Family tree - The simple past tense - Durative past - Simple vs. compound verbs - Arabic in Persian - Exclamatory sentences - Word study
5	- Modals – باید - خواستن – توانستن - The present perfect tense - The past tense and past participle of the verbs - The past perfect - Negation - The auxiliary خواستن - The definite future - Word study – synonyms - Spelling rules

Contents of the Units

unit	a) Topic/Content	b) Function/Task
6	- Three Meals a Day - Daily Routine - A Persian Anecdote	- Extracting information from a Persian menu - Inviting and refusing an invitation - Offering, accepting and declining food - Applying for a part time job - Discussing your daily routine - Deriving basic facts from the stretches of language beyond words and phrases on familiar topics - Understanding the humor of Persian anecdotes
7	- A Birthday Celebration Happy Birthday Song in Persian - Persian proverbs - Persian Idioms - Arabic in Persian - Language Games in Persian	- Planning for a birthday party - Making suggestions - Giving assignments to friends - Expressing surprise and interest - Surprising a friend at his/her birthday - Asking for and giving advice - Talking about preference - Agreeing and disagreeing - Making, agreeing to, and rejecting suggestions - Practicing the Persian birthday song - Doing the word puzzle – Zahedan - Reading the map of the province of Baluchestan and Sista

Contents of the Units

unit	c) Structure
6	- The functions of the pronoun خود - The emphatic and reflexive meanings of خود - The present progressive tense - The past progressive tense - The use of داشتن as an auxiliary verb in Progressive tenses - Deletion of the auxiliary داشتن - Spelling rules - Word study- synonyms, content areas, antonyms - Review of question words - Review of tenses - Review of compound verbs - Sentence connectors, their meanings and functions in sequence of sentence
7	- Word study – کلمه های هم خانواده - Colloquial words in Happy Birthday - Word definition - Categorization of words - Inflection of adjectives - The use of همه - Arabic in Persian – Arabic infinitive - Compound Infinitives with Arabic infinitives - The use of adjectives and nouns as adverbs - Types of adverbs - Coordinated sentences - Subordinate clauses

PREFACE

In the past two decades, competency-based instruction and proficiency testing have received increased attention in the teaching of foreign languages. The joint efforts of major professional organizations, including the American Council on the Teaching of Foreign Languages (ACTFL), Educational Testing Services (ETS), and the Interagency Language Roundtable (ILR), have resulted in the development of guidelines for proficiency-oriented programs and the establishment of national proficiency goals for foreign language instruction.

In the languages of the Middle East, with the exception of Arabic and Hebrew, proficiency guidelines for competency-based instruction and evaluation are not yet available. While the development of proficiency-oriented textbooks in less commonly taught languages, such as Persian, has lagged behind.

An examination of existing Persian textbooks reveals that most are organized around the traditional grammar structure. Grammar lessons are central, and all other materials are geared to support such lessons. Reading selections used in these textbooks are mostly from classical sources that contain archaic forms and styles no longer used in contemporary Persian. Consequently, a common tendency is to disregard discourse and speech patterns of contemporary usage.

Current demands and continued advances in methodology call for the development of new instructional materials. Persian should be taught covering the four language skills (listening, speaking, reading, writing), and also introduce the learner to Persian culture.

COURSE DESCRIPTION

The course is designed for classroom instruction with a corresponding amount of independent study/homework time that occurs outside of class. It is designed to teach the basic skills of language, which encompass understanding, speaking and reading. The accompanying manual – *Persian Handwriting* with CD-ROM – provide a systematic presentation of the script. For better comprehension of spoken Persian, both formal and informal styles are presented from the beginning.

The corpus of Persian presented in this textbook is selected for use in communicative activities, which occur outside the classroom in daily living situations. The lessons deal with topics such as asking questions, making requests, expressing disagreement, extending invitations, and other interactions for which particular linguistic forms are employed. The focus is on studying the language in authentic contexts. Pronunciation, basic sentence structures, and basic vocabulary are used and practiced in the context of conversations, reading lessons, and written assignments.

Spoken Persian is emphasized throughout the course and is practiced through dialogues, role-playing and additional meaningful activities to stimulate conversation in colloquial Persian. Work in spoken Persian continues through the course, and the level of difficulty of spoken Persian increases as successive lessons are mastered. Particular attention is paid to the differences that exist between the colloquial and the formal (written) style of Persian. Although the two styles have a great deal in common, there are differences of which learners should become aware from the start.

The lessons presented in Book One of the series are intended for beginning level of Persian studies at level zero/ o+/1. The materials have been carefully laid out and sequenced in the order of difficulty.

THE SYLLABUS

The basic course for which this syllabus has been prepared consists of seven units. Each unit may include:

1. Vocabulary
2. Dialogues
3. Explanatory notes
4. Situation cards
5. Reading lessons
6. Activities to promote oral communication
7. CD-ROM and DVD disks for practice in the language lab or at home
8. Work sheets (to be done at home)

All of the dialogues are short and can be learned quickly. Each dialogue deals with a familiar situation that is likely to be encountered in everyday conversation. The conversations are designed to be learned with minimum effort, especially when learned in conjunction with the accompanying audio tapes.

The explanatory notes deal mainly with the writing system, pronunciation, and the cultural content of the lessons. They are also intended to provide answers to the commonly-asked questions about these and other features of the lessons

Assignments are intended to give students an opportunity to review the materials presented in the units in various ways. In preparing the assignments, students are advised to keep the following points in mind:

1. Carefully follow the directions given in the book. At every step students will be prompted just what to do next. For example, instructions will be given as to which audio track to listen to, which sentences to copy, which questions to answer, when to take a self test, and which papers to prepare at home for corrections.

2. Persian cannot be learned overnight. Once the course has begun, it would be best to spend some time on the lessons every day. Spending an hour or two daily will yield the most benefit from the course. On the other hand, if the coursework is not attended to regularly and steadily, previous lessons will be easily forgotten and more time will be needed for review.
3. Most functions, grammatical structures and strategies occur at several points in the book and the accompanying materials. It will be especially helpful to conduct frequent focused reviews of the useful expressions, grammatical structures, specific functions and strategies.

Beginning with Unit One, short selections for practice in reading are presented. For the most part, these lessons contain familiar vocabulary and grammatical structures utilized in the dialogues. Occasionally, new expressions in the reading lessons are introduced. In reading, particular attention needs to be given to the differences that exist between the informal spoken style and the formal written style of Persian. Although the two styles have a great deal in common, there are differences. Often what is heard in spoken Persian is not recorded in written Persian in exactly the same way. Some of the differences in pronunciation, usage and word order will be demonstrated in this book.

THE ACCOMPANYING TEACHING AIDS

Audio Tapes

All materials presented in this manual are recorded on audiotape, with the exception of some of the exercises. On the tape, a conversation or reading lesson is first presented in its entirety. Then the speakers pronounce each sentence with pauses for repetition. Different native speakers have recorded the tapes in order to expose the students to a variety of voices. This variety helps students understand the language better.

Flashcards

For active recall of vocabulary and practice on recognition of letters of the alphabet and spelling, Persian flashcards have been designed. They serve as word cues in oral drills, but may be used for review purposes as well. The easiest and most common use of these cards is to "flash" them briefly for the class to read.

Situation Cards

Situation cards are intended to help the students initiate conversation. The English instructions on the cards are not to be translated into Persian. They are guidelines for generating meaningful dialogue in Persian about the specific situations indicated on the cards. This type of role-playing encourages students to ask and answer questions.

Persian Handwriting

A systemic presentation of the script has been placed in the accompanying writing manual. The 240 page, soft bound ***Persian Handwriting*** and accompanying CD-ROM make it possible for the students of Persian to enhance their understanding and ability with the Persian writing system.

NAMING THE LANGUAGE

Persian فارسی

In the past few years, the word Farsi has often been used in English rather than the better-known and more correct word 'Persian.' The use of the word "Farsi" has caused some confusion and should be avoided. A few years ago, the Society of Iranian Studies issued a resolution against the use of this word in English that reads as follows:

The Society for Iranian Studies, which is the professional organization of teachers and students in the field, would like to draw your attention to the correct English term for the language spoken by most Iranians, which is Persian. In recent years some English speakers to refer to the Persian language have used the word 'Farsi'. This is confusing and has no basis in the history of the English language. The English word is Persian. 'Farsi' is the Persian word for that language as 'Français' is the French word for the language spoken in France and 'Deutsche' is the German word for the language spoken in Germany. We are not sure where this usage of 'Farsi' arose, but the Society urges English speakers to use the word 'Persian' when referring to the language in question.

PERSIAN AS AN INDO-EUROPEAN LANGUAGE

Persian belongs to the Iranian branch of the Indo-European family of languages. The Iranian branch includes Pashtu, Kurdish, Baluchi, Taleshi, Asi, etc. English and Persian are distantly related languages - in that they are both branches of the Indo-European language family. Similarities between the two languages exist in word formation, syntax, and phonological rules. These similarities are also helpful in learning Persian especially in the initial stages.

ACKNOWLEDGEMENTS

I would like to express my special thanks to colleagues who adopted the earlier edition of this book in their Persian program and encouraged me in the development of this program. The insight gained from suggestions and discussions has been of great value and assistance in preparing the present edition of this book.

This curriculum has its roots in teaching Persian to Peace Corps volunteers long before we tried to implement proficiency in teaching Persian in university programs. Among those who kindly contributed valuable suggestions and critical comments, I should mention my mentor the late Professor M. A. Jazayery of the University of Texas at Austin, who introduced me to the principles of teaching Persian as a foreign language upon which proficiency-based instruction is founded.

Heartfelt thanks to reviewers and class testers whose critical and favorable comments lie at the core of this program. Appreciation goes to colleagues at other institutions including: Ahmad Karimi-Hakkak (University of Maryland); Latifeh Hagigi (University of California, Los Angeles); Dalia Yarshapour (Harvard University); Soheila Amirsoleimani, (University of Utah); Anousha Sadighi (Portland State University); Firoozeh Papan-Matin (University of Washington); Mohammad Esmaili (University of Maryland); Afteh Oliaie (University of Wisconsin).

I am also grateful to Dr. Mehdi Khorami (New York University) for his valuable contributions in the development of the accompanying CD-ROM for ***Persian Handwriting,*** and my gratitude and love to my nieces -Mojdeh and Nazanin Marashi - for their inspired artwork and assistance in Iran.

SKILL-LEVEL DESCRIPTIONS

The following skill levels as described by the Interagency Language Roundtable (ILR) characterize proficiency in listening, speaking reading, and writing skills.

Listening 0 (No Proficiency)

No practical understanding of the spoken language. Understanding is limited to occasional isolated words with essentially no ability to comprehend communication.

Listening 0 + (Memorized Proficiency)

Sufficient comprehension to understand a number of memorized utterances in areas of immediate need. Can understand slightly longer utterances than at Level 0, but requires frequent long pauses between understood phrases and repeated requests on the listener's part for repetition. Understands with reasonable accuracy only when short memorized utterances or formulae are involved. Misunderstandings arise due to ignoring or inaccurately hearing sounds or word endings (both inflectional and non-inflectional), thus distorting the original meaning. Can understand only with difficulty even persons (such as teachers) who are used to speaking with nonnative speakers. Can best understand those statements in which context strongly supports the utterance meaning. Gets some main ideas.

Listening 1 (Elementary Proficiency)

Sufficient comprehension to understand utterances about basic survival needs and minimum courtesy and travel requirements. In areas of immediate need or on very familiar topics, can understand simple

questions and answers, simple statements, and very simple face-to-face conversations in a standard dialect. These must often be delivered more clearly than normal and at a rate slower than normal, with frequent repetitions or paraphrases (that is, by a native used to dealing with foreigners). Once learned, these sentences can be varied for similar level vocabulary and grammar and still be understood. In the majority of utterances, misunderstandings arise due to overlooked or misunderstood syntax and other grammatical clues. Comprehend thoroughly subject matter that is highly dependent on cultural knowledge or is outside his general experience and not accompanied by explanation. Text-types include news stories similar to wire service reports or internal news items in major periodicals, routine correspondence, general reports, and technical material in his professional field; all of these may include hypothesis, argumentation, and supported opinions. Misreading rare. Almost always able to interpret material correctly, relate ideas, and "read between the lines" (that is, understand the writers' implicit intents in texts of the above types). Can get the gist of more sophisticated texts but may be unable to detect or understand subtlety and nuance. Rarely has to pause over or reread general vocabulary. However, may experience some difficulty with unusually complex structure and low-frequency idioms.

Comprehension areas include basic needs such as meals, lodging, transportation, time, and simple directions (including both route instructions and orders from officials such as customs agents and police). Understands main ideas.

Listening 1 + (Elementary Proficiency, Plus)

Sufficient comprehension to understand short conversations about all survival needs and limited social demands. Developing flexibility evident in understanding expanded to a range of circumstances beyond immediate survival needs. Shows spontaneity by speed of understanding, although consistency of understanding is uneven. Limited vocabulary range necessitates repetition for understanding. Understands more common time forms and most question forms, as well as some word

order patterns, but miscommunication still occurs with more complex patterns. Cannot sustain understanding of coherent structures in longer utterances or in unfamiliar situations. Understanding of descriptions and the giving of precise information are limited. Aware of basic cohesive features such as pronouns and verb inflections, but many are unreliably understood, especially if less immediate in reference. Understanding is largely limited to a series of short, discrete utterances. Still has to ask for utterances to be repeated. Some ability to understand facts.

Speaking O (No Proficiency)

Unable to function in the spoken language. Oral production is limited to occasional isolated words. Has essentially no communicative ability.

Speaking O + (Memorized Proficiency)

Able to satisfy immediate needs using rehearsed utterances. Shows little real autonomy of expression, flexibility, or spontaneity. Can ask questions or make statements with reasonable accuracy only with memorized utterances or formulas. Attempts at creating speech are unsuccessful.

Examples: The individual's vocabulary is usually limited to areas of immediate survival needs. Most utterances are telegraphic; that is, functors (linking words, markers, and the like) are omitted, confused, or distorted. An individual can usually differentiate most significant sounds when produced in isolation, but when sounds are combined in words or groups of words, errors may be frequent. Even with repetition, communication is severely limited even with persons used to dealing with foreigners. Features such as stress, intonation, and tone are usually quite faulty.

Speaking 1 (Elementary Proficiency)

Able to satisfy minimum courtesy requirements and maintain very simple face-to-face conversations on familiar topics. A native speaker must often use slowed speech, repetition, paraphrase, or a combination of these to be understood by this individual. Similarly, the native speaker must strain and employ real-world knowledge to understand even simple statements and questions from this individual. This speaker has a functional, but limited proficiency. Misunderstandings are frequent, but the individual is able to ask for help and to verify comprehension of native speech in face-to-face interaction. The person is unable to produce continuous discourse except with rehearsed material

Examples: Structural accuracy is likely to be random or severely limited. Time concepts are vague. Vocabulary is inaccurate, and its range is very narrow. The individual often speaks with great difficulty. By repeating, such speakers can make themselves understood to native speakers who are in regular contact with foreigners, but there is little precision in the information conveyed. Needs, experience, or training may vary greatly from individual to individual; for example speakers at this level may have encountered quite different vocabulary areas. However, the individual can typically satisfy predictable simple, personal, and accommodation needs; can generally meet courtesy, introduction, and identification requirements; can exchange greetings; and can elicit and provide, for example, predictable skeletal biographical information. He might give information about business hours, explain routine procedures in a limited way, and state in a simple manner what actions will be taken. He is able to formulate some questions even in languages with complicated question constructions. Almost every utterance may be characterized by structure errors and errors in basic grammatical relations. Vocabulary is extremely limited and characteristically does not include modifiers. Pronunciation, stress, and intonation are generally poor, often influenced by another language. Use of structure and vocabulary is highly imprecise.

Speaking 1 + (Elementary Proficiency, Plus)

Can initiate and maintain predictable face-to-face conversations and satisfy limited social demands. He may, however, have little understanding of the social conventions of conversation. The interlocutor is generally required to strain and employ real-world knowledge to understand even some simple speech. The speaker at this level may hesitate and may have to change subjects due to lack of language resources. Range and control of the language are limited. Speech largely consists of a series of short, discrete utterances.

Examples: The individual is able to satisfy most travel and accommodation needs and a limited range of social demands beyond exchange of skeletal biographic information. Speaking ability may extend beyond immediate survival needs. Accuracy in basic grammar relations is evident, although not consistent. May exhibit the more common forms of verb tenses, for example, but may make frequent errors in formation and selection. While some structures are established errors occur in more complex patterns. The individual typically cannot sustain coherent structures in longer utterances or unfamiliar situations. Ability to describe and give precise information is limited. Person, space, and time references are often used incorrectly. Pronunciation is understandable to natives used to dealing with foreigners. Can combine most significant sounds with reasonable comprehensibility, but has difficulty in producing certain sounds in certain positions or in certain combinations. Speech will usually be labored. Frequently has to repeat utterances to be understood by the general public. .

Note: In the following descriptions, a standard set of text-types is associated with each level. The text-type is generally characterized in each descriptive statement.

The word 'read' in the context of these proficiency descriptions, means that the person at a given skill level can thoroughly understand the communicative intent in the text-types described. In the usual case the

reader could be expected to make a full representation, thorough summary, or translation of the text into English. Other useful operations can be performed on written texts that do not require the ability to 'read' as defined above. Examples of such tasks that people of a given skill level may reasonably be expected to perform are provided, when appropriate, in the descriptions.

Reading 0 (No Proficiency)

No practical ability to read the language. Consistently misunderstands or cannot comprehend the written language.

Reading 0 + (Memorized Proficiency)

Can recognize all the letters in the printed version of an alphabetic system and high-frequency elements of a syllabary or character system. Able to read some or all of the following: numbers, isolated words and phrases, personal and place names, street signs, office and shop designations. The above often interpreted inaccurately.

Reading 1 (Elementary Proficiency)

Sufficient comprehension to read very simple, connected, written material in a form equivalent to usual printing or typescript. Can read either representations of familiar formulaic verbal exchanges or simple language containing only the highest frequency structural patterns and vocabulary, including shared international vocabulary terms and cognates (when appropriate). Able to read and understand known language elements that have been recombined in new ways to achieve different meanings at a similar level of complexity. Texts may include simple narratives of routine behavior; highly predictable descriptions of persons, places, or things; and explanations of geography and government such as those simplified for tourists. Some misunderstandings of simple texts possible. Can get some main ideas and locate prominent items of professional significance in more complex texts. Can identify general subject matter in some authentic texts. (Has

been coded R-1 in some nonautomated applications.)

Reading 1 + (Elementary Proficiency, Plus)

Sufficient comprehension to understand simple discourse in printed form for informative social purposes. Can read material such as announcements of public events, simple prose containing biographical information or narration of events, and straightforward newspaper headlines. Can guess at unfamiliar vocabulary if highly contextualized, but with difficulty in unfamiliar contexts. Can get some main ideas and locate routine information of professional significance in more complex texts. Can follow essential points of written discussion at an elementary level in topics in his special professional field. In commonly taught languages, the individual may not control the structure well. For example, basic grammatical relations are often misinterpreted, and temporal reference may rely primarily on lexical items as time indicators. Has some difficulty with the cohesive factors in the discourse, such as matching pronouns with referents. May have to read materials several times for understanding.

(See the skill level description of the higher level of proficiency in *Proficiency in Persian, Books Two and Three.)*